"This series is a tremendous resource for those wanting to study and teach the Bible with an understanding of how the gospel is woven throughout Scripture. Here are gospel-minded pastors and scholars doing gospel business from all the Scriptures. This is a biblical and theological feast preparing God's people to apply the entire Bible to all of life with heart and mind wholly committed to Christ's priorities."

> **BRYAN CHAPELL,** President Emeritus, Covenant Theological Seminary; Senior Pastor, Grace Presbyterian Church, Peoria, Illinois

"Mark Twain may have smiled when he wrote to a friend, 'I didn't have time to write you a short letter, so I wrote you a long letter.' But the truth of Twain's remark remains serious and universal, because well-reasoned, compact writing requires extra time and extra hard work. And this is what we have in the Crossway Bible study series *Knowing the Bible*. The skilled authors and notable editors provide the contours of each book of the Bible as well as the grand theological themes that bind them together as one Book. Here, in a 12-week format, are carefully wrought studies that will ignite the mind and the heart."

> **R. KENT HUGHES,** Visiting Professor of Practical Theology, Westminster Theological Seminary

"*Knowing the Bible* brings together a gifted team of Bible teachers to produce a high-quality series of study guides. The coordinated focus of these materials is unique: biblical content, provocative questions, systematic theology, practical application, and the gospel story of God's grace presented all the way through Scripture."

> **PHILIP G. RYKEN,** President, Wheaton College

"These *Knowing the Bible* volumes provide a significant and very welcome variation on the general run of inductive Bible studies. This series provides substantial instruction, as well as teaching through the very questions that are asked. *Knowing the Bible* then goes even further by showing how any given text links with the gospel, the whole Bible, and the formation of theology. I heartily endorse this orientation of individual books to the whole Bible and the gospel, and I applaud the demonstration that sound theology was not something invented later by Christians, but is right there in the pages of Scripture."

> **GRAEME L. GOLDSWORTHY,** former lecturer, Moore Theological College; author, *According to Plan*, *Gospel and Kingdom*, *The Gospel in Revelation*, and *Gospel and Wisdom*

"What a gift to earnest, Bible-loving, Bible-searching believers! The organization and structure of the Bible study format presented through the *Knowing the Bible* series is so well conceived. Students of the Word are led to understand the content of passages through perceptive, guided questions, and they are given rich insights and application all along the way in the brief but illuminating sections that conclude each study. What potential growth in depth and breadth of understanding these studies offer! One can only pray that vast numbers of believers will discover more of God and the beauty of his Word through these rich studies."

> **BRUCE A. WARE,** Professor of Christian Theology, The Southern Baptist Theological Seminary

KNOWING THE BIBLE

J. I. Packer, Theological Editor
Dane C. Ortlund, Series Editor
Lane T. Dennis, Executive Editor

• • • • • •

Genesis	Psalms	Jonah, Micah, and Nahum	Ephesians
Exodus	Proverbs		Philippians
Leviticus	Ecclesiastes	Haggai, Zechariah, and Malachi	Colossians and Philemon
Numbers	Song of Solomon		
Deuteronomy	Isaiah	Matthew	1–2 Thessalonians
Joshua	Jeremiah	Mark	1–2 Timothy and Titus
Judges	Lamentations, Habakkuk, and Zephaniah	Luke	
Ruth and Esther		John	Hebrews
1–2 Samuel		Acts	James
1–2 Kings	Ezekiel	Romans	
1–2 Chronicles	Daniel	1 Corinthians	1–2 Peter and Jude
Ezra and Nehemiah	Hosea	2 Corinthians	1–3 John
Job	Joel, Amos, and Obadiah	Galatians	Revelation

• • • • • •

J. I. PACKER was the former Board of Governors' Professor of Theology at Regent College (Vancouver, BC). Dr. Packer earned his DPhil at the University of Oxford. He is known and loved worldwide as the author of the best-selling book *Knowing God*, as well as many other titles on theology and the Christian life. He served as the General Editor of the ESV Bible and as the Theological Editor for the *ESV Study Bible*.

LANE T. DENNIS is CEO of Crossway, a not-for-profit publishing ministry. Dr. Dennis earned his PhD from Northwestern University. He is Chair of the ESV Bible Translation Oversight Committee and Executive Editor of the *ESV Study Bible*.

DANE C. ORTLUND (PhD, Wheaton College) serves as senior pastor of Naperville Presbyterian Church in Naperville, Illinois. He is an editor for the Knowing the Bible series and the Short Studies in Biblical Theology series, and is the author of several books, including *Gentle and Lowly: The Heart of Christ for Sinners and Sufferers*.

ACTS

A 12-WEEK STUDY

Justin S. Holcomb

:: CROSSWAY®

WHEATON, ILLINOIS

Crossway is a publishing ministry of Good News Publishers.

VP		30	29	28	27	26	25	24	23	22	21
20	19	18	17	16	15	14	13	12	11	10	9

TABLE OF CONTENTS

▲

Series Preface: J. I. Packer and Lane T. Dennis.............................6

Week 1:   Overview...7

Week 2:   You Will Be My Witnesses (Acts 1:1–26) 11

Week 3:   Pentecost (Acts 2:1–47) 19

Week 4:   Growing Witness and Opposition (Acts 3:1–5:42) 27

Week 5:   Stephen (Acts 6:1–7:60)..35

Week 6:   Saul (Acts 8:1–9:31) 43

Week 7:   The Gospel to the Gentiles (Acts 9:32–12:25)...................51

Week 8:   Paul and Barnabas Are Sent (Acts 13:1–14:28) 59

Week 9:   The Jerusalem Council (Acts 15:1–35).........................67

Week 10: Paul's Second and Third Missionary Journeys 75
          (Acts 15:36–21:16)

Week 11: The Gospel Goes to Rome (Acts 21:17–28:31)...................83

Week 12: Summary and Conclusion 91

SERIES PREFACE

KNOWING THE BIBLE, as the series title indicates, was created to help readers know and understand the meaning, the message, and the God of the Bible. Each volume in the series consists of 12 units that progressively take the reader through a clear, concise study of that book of the Bible. In this way, any given volume can fruitfully be used in a 12-week format either in group study, such as in a church-based context, or in individual study. Of course, these 12 studies could be completed in fewer or more than 12 weeks, as convenient, depending on the context in which they are used.

Each study unit gives an overview of the text at hand before digging into it with a series of questions for reflection or discussion. The unit then concludes by highlighting the gospel of grace in each passage ("Gospel Glimpses"), identifying whole-Bible themes that occur in the passage ("Whole-Bible Connections"), and pinpointing Christian doctrines that are affirmed in the passage ("Theological Soundings").

The final component to each unit is a section for reflecting on personal and practical implications from the passage at hand. The layout provides space for recording responses to the questions proposed, and we think readers need to do this to get the full benefit of the exercise. The series also includes definitions of key words. These definitions are indicated by a note number in the text and are found at the end of each chapter.

Lastly, to help understand the Bible in this deeper way, we urge readers to use the ESV Bible and the *ESV Study Bible*, which are available in various print and digital formats, including online editions at esv.org. The Knowing the Bible series is also available online.

May the Lord greatly bless your study as you seek to know him through knowing his Word.

J. I. Packer
Lane T. Dennis

WEEK 1: OVERVIEW

▲

> ## Getting Acquainted

Acts is the story of God's grace flooding out to the world. Nothing is more prominent in Acts than the spread of the gospel.[1] Jesus promises a geographic expansion at the outset, and Acts follows the news of his death and resurrection as it spreads from a small group of disciples in Jerusalem to Judea, Samaria, and the faraway capital of Rome.

Through the repeated preaching of the gospel[2] to different people groups, the gospel of grace draws them in, constitutes them as the church centered on the grace of Jesus, and then sends them out in mission[3] to the world. Acts is a historical account of how the resurrection of Jesus changes everything through the birth of the early church.

God is clearly central to the gospel's expansion. He is at the heart of the gospel message and, through the Holy Spirit, he is responsible for its remarkable growth. The gospel expands not through human strength but through the power of God over significant barriers of geography, ethnicity, culture, language, gender, wealth, persecutions, weaknesses, suffering, sickness, and imprisonments. Many of these barriers appear so inviolable that, when the gospel is preached to a new segment of society, riots ensue. But Acts makes clear that no one is beyond the scope of God's saving power, nor is anyone exempt from the need for God's redeeming grace. (For further background, see the *ESV Study* Bible, pages 2073–2079, or visit esv.org.)

Placing It in the Larger Story

Acts shows that the new Christian movement is not a fringe sect, but the culmination of God's plan of redemption. What was seen only as shadows in the Old Testament, God reveals finally and fully through Jesus Christ. The book of Acts does not primarily provide human patterns to emulate or avoid. Instead, it repeatedly calls us to reflect upon the work of God, fulfilled in Jesus Christ, establishing the church by the power of the Holy Spirit.

The gospel's expansion is the culmination of what God has been doing since the beginning. Acts consistently grounds salvation in the ancient purpose of God, which comes to fruition at God's own initiative. This reveals God to be the great benefactor who pours out blessings on all people. Even the opportunity to repent is God's gift.

Key Verse

"But you will receive power when the Holy Spirit has come upon you, and you will be my witnesses in Jerusalem and in all Judea and Samaria, and to the end of the earth" (Acts 1:8).

Date and Historical Background

Acts is the second part of a two-volume work, with the Gospel of Luke being the first volume. Neither book names its author, however the Lukan authorship of Luke–Acts is affirmed by both external evidence (church tradition) and internal evidence. Church tradition supporting Luke as the author is both early (from the mid-2nd century AD) and for over a century and a half unanimous (it was never doubted until the 19th century). The "we" sections of Acts (16:10–17; 20:5–21:18; 27:1–28:16) reveal that the author was a companion of Paul and participated in the events described in those sections. So the author of Acts was one of Paul's companions listed in his letters written during those periods (Luke is listed in Col. 4:14; 2 Tim. 4:11; Philem. 24) and not one of the men referred to in the third person in the "we" sections (see Acts 20:4–5). It seems clear that the author was from the second generation of the early church, since he was not an "eyewitness" of Jesus' ministry (Luke 1:2), and was a Gentile (Eusebius, *Ecclesiastical History* 3.4.6, says Luke was "by race an Antiochian and a physician by profession"; see Col. 4:14).

A number of scholars date Acts as early as AD 62, a guess based primarily on the abrupt conclusion of the book. Since Acts ends with Paul in Rome under house arrest, awaiting his trial before Caesar (28:30–31), it would seem strange if Luke knew about Paul's release (a proof of his innocence), about his defense before Caesar (fulfilling 27:24), and about his preaching the gospel as far as Spain (see note on 28:30–31), but then did not mention these events at the end of Acts. It seems most likely, then, that the abrupt ending is an indication that Luke completed Acts c. AD 62, before these later events occurred.

Outline

   I. Preparation for Witness (1:1–2:13)

  II. The Witness in Jerusalem (2:14–5:42)

 III. The Witness beyond Jerusalem (6:1–12:25)

 IV. The Witness in Cyprus and Southern Galatia (13:1–14:28)

  V. The Jerusalem Council (15:1–35)

 VI. The Witness in Greece (15:36–18:22)

VII. The Witness in Ephesus (18:23–21:16)

VIII. The Arrest in Jerusalem (21:17–23:35)

 IX. The Witness in Caesarea (24:1–26:32)

  X. The Witness in Rome (27:1–28:31)

As You Get Started . . .

What is your understanding of how Acts relates to the storyline of the New Testament and of the whole Bible? How does it help you to better understand the cultures and people of other New Testament books?

What is your overall understanding of how Acts relates to Luke, knowing that this is part 2 of a two-part narrative? Do you have any sense of what Acts uniquely contributes to that narrative? Do you have any sense of similarities and continuities between Luke and Acts?

How do you understand the contribution of Acts to Christian theology? From your current knowledge of Acts, what do you think this book teaches us about God, the church, the gospel, and other doctrines?

What aspects of Acts have confused you? Are there any specific questions that you hope to resolve through this study of Acts?

As You Finish This Unit . . .

Take a few moments now to ask the Lord to bless you, change you, and help you understand and apply the unique light Acts throws on the gospel to your life.

Definitions

[1] **Gospel** – A common translation for a Greek word meaning "good news," that is, the good news of Jesus Christ and the salvation he made possible by his crucifixion, burial, and resurrection. Gospel with an initial capital letter refers to each of the biblical accounts of Jesus' life on earth (Matthew, Mark, Luke, and John).

[2] **Preach the gospel** – The preaching of Jesus' death and resurrection is central in Acts. The Greek verb, "preach the gospel" (*euangelizo*), occurs more often in this book than in any other in the New Testament. About a third of the book of Acts consists of speeches, and most of these are speeches of Peter or Paul proclaiming the gospel. The good news of the salvation accomplished in Christ and applied by the Holy Spirit extends to the "ends of the earth" through preaching.

[3] **Mission of God** – God's plan of redemption for all of creation, initiated at the beginning and culminating in the life, death, resurrection, and ascension of Jesus Christ and the outpouring of the Spirit at Pentecost. The mission of God is his work to reconcile the world to himself through Jesus Christ by lavishly offering grace to sinners and sufferers.

Week 2: You Will Be My Witnesses

Acts 1:1–26

▲

The Place of the Passage

In this opening chapter of Acts, Luke introduces several important gospel perspectives that recur throughout the rest of the book. Chief among them is that the book of Acts is first and foremost a book about Jesus. He is the primary character of the book and the focus of all its events. Acts depicts the continuing actions and teachings of Jesus, following his ascension, in a way that no other book of the Bible does. Acts demonstrates that as the budding Christian movement spreads, Jesus himself is at work. The church is Jesus' vehicle to continue his work in the world. In the opening chapter, Jesus promises his disciples the Holy Spirit in power (1:5), commissions them to take the gospel to the "end of the earth" (1:8), ascends into heaven (1:9), and is promised to return again (1:11).

The Big Picture

Acts 1 shows us that the ministry of Jesus did not stop with the Gospels; it is an ongoing work, initiated by Jesus' death, resurrection,[1] and ascension, and thereafter mediated by the Holy Spirit.

Reflection and Discussion

Read through the complete passage for this study, Acts 1:1–26. Then review the questions below concerning this first chapter of Acts and write your notes on them. (For further background, see the *ESV Study Bible*, pages 2080–2082, or visit esv.org.)

1. The Promise of the Holy Spirit and Jesus' Return (1:1–11)

Acts 1:1 addresses "Theophilus" and references a previous book, the Gospel of Luke. Here in the first verse of Acts the work and teachings of Jesus are center stage. Why do you think that is? Why do you think that might be important to what Luke is going to say?

In Acts 1:1 Luke also makes the point that in the Gospel of Luke he wrote about "all that Jesus began to do and teach." What does that phrase imply about the content of Acts?

In Acts 1:6 the disciples ask Jesus, "will you at this time restore the kingdom to Israel?" Jesus responds by telling them that it is not for them to know the times or seasons, but rather "you will receive power when the Holy Spirit has come upon you, and you will be my witnesses in Jerusalem and in all Judea and

Samaria, and to the end of the earth" (1:8). How does Jesus' response challenge and expand the disciples' thinking and understanding of the gospel?

How might Acts 1:8 provide a structural and thematic template for the rest of the book? Where do you see this?

2. Matthias Chosen to Be among the Apostles (1:12–26)

One way to summarize the message of Acts is that it is the story of the continuing work of Jesus through his witnesses, despite significant internal and external oppositions and barriers. Throughout Acts we will see that God oftentimes directly uses these oppositions to advance the gospel. This latter half of the first chapter of Acts describes how this was true even for the first disciples of Jesus. Judas, one of their very own, betrayed Jesus. But we see that Jesus uses significant barriers, oppositions, and even sins like this to advance his kingdom. How do we see this in Acts 1:12–26 and the choosing of Matthias? Can you think of any other Old Testament or New Testament passages that also illustrate this?

Read through the following three sections on *Gospel Glimpses*, *Whole-Bible Connections*, and *Theological Soundings*. Then take time to consider the *Personal Implications* these sections may have for you.

Gospel Glimpses

WITNESSES. The primary task of the people of God is to bear witness to his great deeds. For the first disciples, they quite literally were charged to bear witness to the risen Christ, whom they had seen with their eyes (see 1 John 1:1–3). This witness would begin in Jerusalem, but would spiral outward in concentric circles to "the end of the earth" (1:8; compare Isa. 49:6). Jesus does not command his disciples to perform certain rituals, to act according to certain rules, or to refrain from certain activities. He promises them that they would testify to his power when the Holy Spirit came upon them. This is not a new concept: God has always desired that his people would be witnesses to his greatness. "I have redeemed you," God says in Isaiah. "'You are my witnesses,' declares the LORD, 'and my servant whom I have chosen, that you may know and believe me and understand that I am he" (Isa. 43:1, 10; compare Isa. 43:12; 44:8).

KINGDOM OF GOD. The disciples ask Jesus about the restoration of "the kingdom to Israel" (1:6), expecting and hoping that Jesus' reign will apply to their current national identity. Jesus corrects them by patiently pointing them to the kingdom of God,[2] the sovereign rule of God over all of creation, not just Israel. He points to the spread of the gospel and their witness: from Jerusalem, to Judea and Samaria, to the ends of the earth (1:8).

Whole-Bible Connections

ALREADY AND NOT YET. Jesus' disciples were hoping that, after all of the wonderful things they had seen in the life, death, and resurrection of the Messiah, God would now bring about the end, the new heavens and new earth promised in Isaiah (65:17–25). But they learn that this is not yet the time to look for Jesus to return. He will return, but in the meantime they will be clothed with power and assurance from his Holy Spirit to go forth and bear fruit in the confidence that God will be with them to the end of the age.

REDEMPTIVE HISTORY. Luke and Acts are narratives about God's plan of salvation. They were written to provide "certainty concerning the things" that had been revealed to Luke and others about what Jesus did and taught (Luke 1:1–4; Acts 1:1–5).

> ## Theological Soundings

TRINITY. Before his ascension, Jesus promises his apostles[3] that they will be empowered by the Holy Spirit to be his witnesses (Acts 1:6–8). According to Jesus, the Father has "fixed" the time for restoring the kingdom "by his own authority" (1:7); the apostles "will receive power when the Holy Spirit has come" upon them (1:8); and they will be Jesus' "witnesses" (1:8). We see here all three persons of the Trinity—Father, Son, and Spirit—who are equal in nature but distinct in role and relationship. Broadly speaking, Christian theology teaches that the Father orchestrates salvation, the Son accomplishes salvation, and the Spirit applies salvation.

THE WORK OF THE HOLY SPIRIT. The Spirit is clearly at work in the key events throughout the history of salvation, including creation, Christ's incarnation, Christ's resurrection, human regeneration, the inspiration and illumination of Scripture, and the believer's sanctification. Throughout Acts, baptism and the gift of the Spirit are closely related. Repentance, forgiveness, water baptism, and reception of the Spirit comprise the basic pattern of conversion. John the Baptist had contrasted his "repentance baptism" with Jesus' "Holy Spirit baptism" (Luke 3:16; Mark 1:8). Jesus points his disciples back to the promise of God to give the Spirit and forward to the fulfillment of this promise in Acts 2.

CHRIST'S ASCENSION. The ascension is Christ's return to heaven from earth (Luke 24:50–51; John 14:2, 12; 16:5, 10, 28; Acts 1:6–11; Eph. 4:8–10; 1 Tim. 3:16; Heb. 4:14; 7:26; 9:24). The incarnation does not cease with Christ's ascension. Jesus lives, now and forever, as true man and true God to mediate between God and man (1 Tim. 2:5). He will come again as he left, fully God and fully man (Acts 1:11). Jesus' ascension is a crucial event in his ministry because it explicitly shows his continual humanity and the permanence of his resurrection. The ascension guarantees that Jesus will always represent humanity before the throne of God as the mediator, intercessor, and advocate for needy humans. Because of the ascension, we can be sure that Jesus' unique resurrection leads the way for the everlasting resurrection of the redeemed. Jesus also ascended to prepare a place for his people (John 14:2–3) and to send the Holy Spirit to fulfill his ministry of witness and empowering (John 16:7), a development which, he said, would be more advantageous for the church than if he had stayed on earth (John 14:12, 17).

CHRIST'S RETURN. Someday Jesus will return in great glory and there will be a definitive, comprehensive acknowledgment that he is Lord over all. He will then judge the living and the dead. All people and forces that oppose him will be vanquished, including death itself (Matt. 25:31; 1 Cor. 15:24–28), "so that at the name of Jesus every knee should bow, in heaven and on earth and under the earth, and every tongue confess that Jesus Christ is Lord, to the glory of God the Father" (Phil. 2:10–11).

Personal Implications

Take time to reflect on the implications of Acts 1:1–26 for your own life today. Make notes below on the personal implications for your walk with the Lord of the (1) *Gospel Glimpses*, (2) *Whole-Bible Connections*, (3) *Theological Soundings*, and (4) this passage as a whole.

1. Gospel Glimpses

2. Whole-Bible Connections

3. Theological Soundings

4. Acts 1:1–26

Take a moment now to ask for the Lord's blessing and help as you continue in this study of Acts. Take a moment also to look back through this unit of study, to reflect on some key things that the Lord may be teaching you—and perhaps to highlight and underline these things to review again in the future.

Definitions

[1] **Resurrection** – The impartation of new, eternal bodily life to a dead person at the end of time (or, in the case of Jesus, on the third day after his death). This new life is not a temporary resuscitation of the body (as in the case of Lazarus; John 11:1–44) but a transformation or reconstruction of the body that is permanent (1 Cor. 15:35–58). Both the righteous and the wicked will be resurrected, the former to eternal life and the latter to judgment and the living death to which condemnation leads (John 5:29).

[2] **Kingdom of God** – The sovereign rule of God. At the present time, the fallen, sinful world does not belong to the kingdom of God, since it does not submit to God's rule. Instead, God's kingdom can be found in heaven and among his people (Matt. 6:9–10; Luke 17:20–21). After Christ returns, however, the kingdoms of the world will become the kingdom of God (Rev. 11:15). Then all people will, either willingly or regretfully, acknowledge his sovereignty (Phil. 2:9–11). Even the natural world will be transformed to operate in perfect harmony with God (Rom. 8:19–23).

[3] **Apostle** – Means "one who is sent" and refers to one who is an official representative of another. In the NT, the word refers specifically to those whom Jesus chose to represent him.

WEEK 3: PENTECOST

Acts 2:1–47

The Place of the Passage

In Acts 2 Jesus' promise of the Spirit becomes a reality as the Spirit descends on the disciples at Pentecost. The disciples "began to speak in other tongues" (2:4), and devout Jews from many nations were amazed, "because each one was hearing them speak in his own language" (v. 6). God thus shows that the gospel is breaking through linguistic barriers and going to all nations, and then Peter stands up and, in the first recorded sermon in Acts, explains how Pentecost is the glorious and long-anticipated fulfillment of God's plan of redemption that has been in place since the beginning. Through Peter's sermon we see the most prominent theme of Acts: the gospel of Jesus will go out to the nations, through the witness of his disciples and the enabling of the Holy Spirit.

The Big Picture

In Acts 2:1–47 Jesus' disciples are filled with the Holy Spirit so that they are enabled to be Jesus' witnesses to the world.

▶ Reflection and Discussion

Read through the complete passage for this study, Acts 2:1–47. Then review the questions below concerning Pentecost and write your notes on them. (For further background, see the *ESV Study Bible*, pages 2082–2086, or visit esv.org.)

1. The Coming of the Holy Spirit (2:1–13)

Acts 2:2–3 describes the filling and presence of the Spirit as a mighty wind and fire. Considering passages like Exodus 13 and Ezekiel 1, what is the significance of the Spirit appearing and being described in this way?

In 2:5–13 the disciples speak in other tongues, and the resident foreigners "hear them telling in [their] own tongues the mighty works of God" (Acts 2:11). This miraculous communication did not depend on their education (which was minimal, among "these ... Galileans"; v. 7) nor eloquence, but on the movement of God's Spirit. Where else in Scripture do you see the power of God working despite or through human weakness?

2. Peter's Sermon (2:14–41)

In Acts 2:14–21 Peter starts his gospel presentation with a citation from Joel 2:28–32. Joel says God's Spirit will be poured out in the last days, the days before the final judgment (the "day of the Lord"). It is clear that Peter is saying the "last days" have begun. What does Peter's quote from Joel 2 say will happen?

In Acts 2:23 we see that God is so sovereign and creative that what was intended for evil he uses for his redemptive plan. God both foreknew and foreordained that Jesus would be crucified, yet that still did not absolve of responsibility those who contributed to his death, for Peter goes on to say, "*you* crucified and killed" him. Read Genesis 50:20. Where else in Scripture do you see a clear teaching of God's sovereignty over world events and human responsibility for evil deeds?

In Acts 2:34–35 Peter cites Psalm 110 and refers to Jesus being at God's "right hand." Jesus also refers to himself as being at the "right hand" (Matt. 22:44; 26:64; Mark 12:36; 14:62; Luke 20:42; 22:69). Read Psalms 16:11; 17:7; 98:1; 139:10; and Romans 8:34 regarding the right hand of God. Considering these passages, what does it mean for Jesus to be at the "right hand" of God?

21

Peter finishes his speech in 2:36 with a short summary of his message: Jesus is "Lord[1] and Christ."[2] Throughout his speech Peter provides a number of different points of evidence for the lordship of Jesus. What evidence does Peter point to?

3. The Spirit at Work in the Disciples (2:42–47)

The grace of God is fruitful and effective, and we see God taking the initiative to spread his grace to ever-expanding numbers of people. Considering Acts 2:42–47, what happens when God works in these first believers individually and collectively?

Read through the following three sections on *Gospel Glimpses*, *Whole-Bible Connections*, and *Theological Soundings*. Then take time to consider the *Personal Implications* these sections may have for you.

Gospel Glimpses

FOR ALL WHO ARE FAR OFF. Jesus promised that the gospel would spread to the end of the earth, and Peter proclaims that "the promise is . . . for all who are far off" (Acts 2:39). The gospel is not confined by geographical boundaries but is universal in scope. But "far off" is not just geographical: by his death and resurrection, Jesus Christ has reconciled to himself all of us who were formerly "far off" from God and from one another. No one is so far removed that God cannot redeem them.

GOD INITIATES. When the celebration of Pentecost comes, Acts 2:1, 5 places 120 of the disciples (1:15) together in Jerusalem. Acts 2:2 then says "and suddenly there came from heaven." The direction of agency is important. While often in non-Christian religion humans must first do the equivalent of speaking in other tongues (mysterious incantations, complicated rites, elaborately altered behavior) in order to lure the gods into visitation, at Pentecost God's Spirit rushes into the scene of his own accord: the apostles are just waiting. Pentecost illustrates the fact that God is the initiator of our salvation; he comes to us independent of our control.

Whole-Bible Connections

BABEL. Following the tower-building at Babel, the nations of the earth were divided by language, unable to come together as a result of their rebellion against God (Gen. 11:1–9). Already in God's redemptive acts of the Old Testament, however, he singled out the Jewish nation in order to mediate blessing to all nations (Gen. 12:1–3; Ex. 19:6). Yet in the ministry of the prophets, the good news of God's grace was communicated only in the Hebrew language. With the outpouring of the Holy Spirit at Pentecost, though, the curse of Babel begins to unravel. No longer is the gospel confined to the Hebrew language; it is available directly to all nations and all languages. The restored order of God's kingdom begins to break into the dark and confused world of sin. Pentecost is, in a sense, a magnificent reversal of Babel.

PENTECOST. Pentecost is the New Testament name for the second of the annual harvest festivals, the "Feast of Weeks," coming 50 days after Passover. It was a one-day festival celebrating the wheat harvest (Ex. 23:16; Lev. 23:15–21; Deut. 16:9–12). Like other celebrations in the Old Testament, the Feast of Weeks was associated with the renewal of the covenant made with Noah and then with Moses. In later Judaism, Pentecost was associated with the day when the law was given at Mount Sinai, so it is significant that God chose to send the Holy Spirit at Pentecost.

Theological Soundings

SALVATION HISTORY. Peter begins his famous Pentecost sermon with an extensive reference to the Old Testament, focused on a citation from the prophet Joel, who predicted that God's Spirit would be poured out in the last days, the days before the final judgment (the "day of the Lord"). According to Peter, the last days have begun. This "new religion" is actually the continuation of what God has been doing through Israel all along. Better yet, this God made promises years ago that these "last days" would come, and at Pentecost God was demonstrating that he is faithful and powerful to keep his promises. As he promised, God is pouring out his Spirit on all flesh—men and women, young and old, Jew and Gentile. God is mercifully and joyfully calling all people to salvation.

LORDSHIP OF JESUS. In Peter's first sermon, an important theological teaching comes into view: Jesus is Lord (Acts 2:36; compare Rom. 10:9; 1 Cor. 12:3). This simple statement poses a fundamental challenge both to the Jews and to the Romans. The Jews, entrenched in their strict version of monotheism, reject the claim of Jesus' lordship as blasphemy. They simply cannot conceive of the one true God coming to earth as a man, especially one who was scorned, mistreated, and killed. A crucified God is a stumbling block and folly (1 Cor. 1:23). Similarly, Jesus' lordship presents an explicit defiance of the Roman political system, which was founded on the supremacy of Caesar as Lord.

HUMAN SIN. Peter tells his listeners, "Repent and be baptized every one of you in the name of Jesus Christ for the forgiveness of your sins" (Acts 2:38). Sin is anything (whether thoughts, actions, or attitudes) that does not express or conform to the holy character of God as shown forth in his moral law. According to the Bible, "all have sinned and fall short of the glory of God" (Rom. 3:23), and "the wages of sin is death" (Rom. 6:23). Only the death and resurrection of Jesus Christ has opened up the way for the forgiveness of sins.

▶ Personal Implications

Take time to reflect on the implications of Acts 2 for your own life today. Consider what you have learned that might lead you to praise God, repent of sin, and trust in his gracious promises. Make notes below on the personal implications for your walk with the Lord of the (1) *Gospel Glimpses*, (2) *Whole-Bible Connections*, (3) *Theological Soundings*, and (4) this passage as a whole.

1. Gospel Glimpses

2. Whole-Bible Connections

3. Theological Soundings

4. Acts 2:1–47

As You Finish This Unit . . .

Take a moment now to ask for the Lord's blessing and help as you continue in this study of Acts. Take a moment also to look back through this unit of study, to reflect on some key things that the Lord may be teaching you—and perhaps to highlight and underline these things to review again in the future.

Definitions

[1] **Lord** – Someone superior in authority or status to another, similar to "master." It is a common translation for several different Hebrew titles for God in the OT, and in the NT it refers to Jesus. When spelled in the OT with small capital letters (Lord) it translates Hebrew *Yahweh* (*YHWH*), "I am," the personal name of God.

[2] **Christ** – Transliteration of the Greek for "anointed one" (equivalent to Hebrew *Messiah*). The term is used throughout the NT as a title for Jesus, indicating his role as Messiah and Savior.

WEEK 4: GROWING WITNESS AND OPPOSITION

Acts 3:1–5:42

The Place of the Passage

The first three chapters of Acts form a triad, focused on the Spirit and the empowerment for witnessing to the name of Jesus that the Spirit will bring. Chapter 1 was waiting for the Spirit, chapter 2 marked the coming of the Spirit, and now chapter 3 shows the apostles being empowered by the Spirit. The work of the Holy Spirit at Pentecost begins to ripple throughout Jerusalem and the new church, empowering miraculous healings and bold preaching of the gospel. The church continues to grow and experience tremendous blessing, but a new theme is introduced: significant opposition. Chapter 4 marks the first persecution, a topic that will continue through to and reach its culmination in the stoning of Stephen (ch. 7). From chapter 4 on, Acts will illustrate the diametrically opposed systems of the "world" and the lordship of Jesus Christ. The apostles are threatened, jailed, and beaten, and conflict arises even from within. Despite the rising opposition, the message of Acts 3–5 is clear: the gospel will advance because God is at work.

The Big Picture

Immediately following the outpouring of the Holy Spirit at Pentecost, Acts 3:1–5:42 records the growing church's experience as Jesus' witnesses: Spirit-empowered ministry, and opposition to that ministry.

Reflection and Discussion

Read through the complete passage for this study, Acts 3:1–5:42. Then review the questions below concerning this section of Acts and write your notes on them. (For further background, see the *ESV Study Bible*, pages 2086–2091, or visit esv.org.)

1. The Church Continues to Grow in Jerusalem (3:1–4:31)

After the lame beggar is miraculously healed, how does the crowd respond to this miracle (Acts 3:9–11)? How does the beggar respond (vv. 8, 11)? How do Peter and John respond to the crowd's amazement in verses 12–16?

Consider the number of different names and titles Peter attributes to Jesus in his speech in 3:12–26. What are they, and how does that help you understand Peter's message?

Acts 4:8–12 records Peter's third speech in three chapters, this time before the Jewish rulers and elders. As before, Peter emphasizes the resurrection of Jesus, but this marks the first time the apostles experience overt opposition to the gospel from authorities. How do Peter and John respond (vv. 19–20)? What do they say is their motivation for witness?

After the elders try to silence the apostles, the disciples pray for boldness to speak God's word (4:24–30). In light of the threats from the established powers, it would be understandable for the believers to pray for relief from persecution. Instead they ask for renewed courage to proclaim the word of God. From where are they drawing such confidence? Look at 4:24, 26, and 27–28.

2. Ananias and Sapphira (4:32–5:11)

In 4:32–37, a number of important characteristics of the first community of believers are mentioned. What are the characteristics? Looking at verse 33, what two "great" things empowered this reality?

The account of Ananias and Sapphira (Acts 5:1–11) is one of the most disturbing narratives in the New Testament. It reveals how essential unity within the church is to God, and how seriously God takes deceit that threatens that unity. Examine 5:3–4. What specifically does Peter say Ananias and Sapphira have done wrong?

Thankfully, we do not receive immediate judgment for our sins as Ananias and Sapphira did. Such judgment is rare in Scripture. However, we can be sure that sin will be dealt with, and that the consequence of sin is always death (Rom. 6:23). Jesus did not choose to die for us because our sin was trivial. Our sin was great, but he chose to die for us because his love for us was greater. We have seen in Acts (2:23, 37–39; 3:13–20) that the God who punished Ananias and Sapphira is the same radically merciful God who offers grace even to those who arranged the crucifixion of his Son. Where else in Scripture do you see examples of God's radically merciful grace?

----

3. Opposition Cannot Stop the Gospel (5:12–42)

In Acts 5, the Sanhedrin[1] wants to kill the disciples, and the apostles are beaten for the first time (v. 40). What motivations does the text reveal for the Sanhedrin's actions? Pay attention to verses 17 and 28.

In Acts 5:35–39, the Pharisee Gamaliel gives a speech, and his words in verses 38–39 could be seen as a thematic description of the entire book of Acts. Every time the gospel meets with opposition in Acts, God finds a way to advance the message. Some of the most overt attempts to squelch the movement—like the persecution of the church in Jerusalem—lead to a further expansion of the gospel (see Acts 8:1–4). No one is able to overthrow the gospel, because it is the power of God for salvation, both here in Jerusalem and to the end of the earth (Rom. 1:16).

Confident in God's sovereignty, how do the apostles respond to all that has been done to them (5:41–42)?

Read through the following three sections on *Gospel Glimpses*, *Whole-Bible Connections*, and *Theological Soundings*. Then take time to consider the *Personal Implications* these sections may have for you.

Gospel Glimpses

BLESSING FOR ALL PEOPLE. Speaking at Solomon's Portico (Acts 3:12–26), Peter reminds his Jewish listeners of God's promise to Abraham that, "In your offspring shall all the families of the earth be blessed" (3:25). Jesus is the fulfillment of the promises God made to Abraham, the founder of the nation of Israel, to bless the entire world through his offspring. Now that promised descendant has come, as Peter says, "to bless you by turning every one of you from your wickedness" (v. 26). He urges them to respond by repenting, so that they can receive "refreshing . . . from the presence of the Lord" (v. 20). Though they are guilty of killing the promised Messiah,[2] God is not seeking to punish them but instead wants to bless and restore them.

GOD FOR US. Faced with threats, the believers pray (Acts 4:23–31). They are bold because they know that the effects of evil are fleeting, and those who oppose the gospel are no threat to God, who is always in control. What others intend for evil, God will work for good (Gen. 50:20). The ultimate example of this was the crucifixion of Jesus, which seemed like the final triumph of evil over good. However, Christ's death was part of God's plan to redeem the world (Acts 4:27–28).

Knowing God's tendency to maneuver the plots of people to accomplish his redemptive purposes, we can be bold and trust God. "If God is for us, who can be against us?" (Rom. 8:31). Not even those who decide matters of life and death pose a true threat, for we know the One who has defeated death.

Whole-Bible Connections

THE SUFFERING MESSIAH. That the Christ would suffer and die was a surprise for most of the Jews, and a significant stumbling block to their believing in Jesus as the promised Messiah (1 Cor. 1:23). Peter points out (Acts 3:18) that the suffering of the Messiah should not have been a surprise but was foretold by the prophets. Isaiah spoke of the Messiah as one who "was pierced for our transgressions" and "crushed for our iniquities" (Isa. 53:5). David foreshadowed the suffering of the Messiah in a Psalm that Jesus quoted on the cross: "They have pierced my hands and feet . . . ; they divide my garments among them, and for my clothing they cast lots" (Ps. 22:16–18; compare Matt. 27:35, 46).

JESUS IS THE BETTER MOSES. In Acts 3:22–23, Peter quotes Moses, who spoke of the promised Messiah as one who would be "a prophet like me" (Deut. 18:15, 18). Jesus is a better and truer Moses, like him in many ways but excelling him in others. Like Moses, Jesus—as a baby—is forced to flee the wrath of a king who kills hundreds of infants in an attempt to find him (Matt. 2:1–21; compare Ex. 1:8–2:10). Like Moses, Jesus brings a law for the people of God from a mountaintop (Matthew 5–7; compare Ex. 19:20). Like Moses, Jesus delivers his people from slavery; but whereas Moses' deliverance only saved the Israelites from physical peril, Jesus delivers us from the slavery of sin and death (Gal. 4:4–7; Heb. 2:15). Jesus' "exodus" beyond the cross to the resurrection (see Luke 9:31) allows us to follow him—as a prophet like Moses—to the Promised Land of eternal life.

THE CHIEF CORNERSTONE. In Acts 4:11, Peter points to Jesus fulfilling one of the Psalms: "the stone that the builders rejected has become the cornerstone" (Ps. 118:22; compare Acts 2:25–28, 34–35). Jesus mentioned this prophecy during his earthly ministry (Luke 20:17), and Peter elaborates on it in the first of his letters (1 Pet. 2:4–8). Though rejected by his own people and crucified, Jesus was vindicated when God raised him from the dead. He now occupies the chief position, the cornerstone, around which the entire church is built up.

Theological Soundings

DIVINE SOVEREIGNTY. God is always personally involved with his creation in sustaining and preserving it, and acting within it to bring about his own perfect goals. Everything that takes place is under God's control. He "works all things according to the counsel of his will" (Eph. 1:11). His providential dominion is over all things (Prov. 16:9; 19:21; James 4:13–15), including kings and kingdoms (Prov. 21:1; Dan. 4:25), and the exact times and places in which people live (Acts 17:26). In Acts 4:23–31, God's sovereignty, even in predetermining the crucifixion (vv. 24, 27–28), encourages prayer and confidence (vv. 29–30). Since Jesus reigns supreme, he is the one to approach with our needs.

THE HUMILIATION OF CHRIST. As the church begins to experience persecution, they are fulfilling what Jesus predicted (John 15:18–21). Jesus' life was filled with rejection, loneliness, poverty, persecution, hunger, temptation, suffering, and finally death. Jesus took on a full, complete human nature, including a physical body, so that he could truly represent humanity (Phil. 2:6; Heb. 2:17). His humiliation reached its greatest depth when he gave his life on the cross for sinful human beings. The cross stands at the center of human history as God's supreme act of love (1 John 4:10, 17).

Personal Implications

Take time to reflect on the implications of Acts 3–5 for your own life today. Consider what you have learned that might lead you to praise God, repent of sin, and trust in his gracious promises. Make notes below on the personal implications for your walk with the Lord of the (1) *Gospel Glimpses*, (2) *Whole-Bible Connections*, (3) *Theological Soundings*, and (4) this passage as a whole.

1. Gospel Glimpses

2. Whole-Bible Connections

3. Theological Soundings

4. Acts 3:1–5:42

As You Finish This Unit . . .

Take a moment now to ask for the Lord's blessing and help as you continue in this study of Acts. Take a moment also to look back through this unit of study, to reflect on some key things that the Lord may be teaching you—and perhaps to highlight and underline these things to review again in the future.

Definitions

[1] **Sanhedrin** – Either a local Jewish tribunal ("council," Matt. 5:22; "courts," Matt. 10:17) or the supreme ecclesiastical court in Jerusalem (Matt. 26:59). Jewish leaders belonging to the Sanhedrin included elders, chief priests, and scribes.

[2] **Messiah** – Transliteration of a Hebrew word meaning "anointed one," the equivalent of the Greek word *Christ*. Anointing was regularly given to anyone designated as king or priest. Jesus himself affirmed that he was the Messiah sent from God (Matt. 16:16–17).

WEEK 5: STEPHEN

Acts 6:1–7:60

▲

The Place of the Passage

The young church begins to experience intensified opposition, and one of its new leaders, Stephen, is executed by the religious authorities for charges of blasphemy. This event marks the beginning of serious persecution. Yet even amid the rising opposition, God's power can be seen at work preparing for the gospel to scatter from Jerusalem out to the nations. Beginning with Greek-speaking Jewish Christians in Jerusalem (Acts 6:1–7), the Christian gospel is proclaimed to an ever-widening circle—to Samaria (8:4–25), to an Ethiopian (vv. 26–40), to a Gentile God-fearer (10:1–48), and to the Gentiles of Antioch (11:19–30). Key figures in the outreach are the Hellenists Stephen and Philip, the apostle Peter, and eventually Paul and Barnabas. The stage is then set for Paul's ministry, which will go to the "end of the earth" (1:8).

The Big Picture

Before his death, Stephen eloquently tells the story of Israel to show how Jesus is the culmination of God's redemptive plan and how, even through rejection and persecution, the power of God is advancing.

35

Reflection and Discussion

Read through the complete passage for this study, Acts 6:1–7:60. Then review the questions below concerning this section of Acts and write your notes on them. (For further background, see the *ESV Study Bible*, pages 2092–2096, or visit esv.org.)

1. Seven Chosen to Serve (6:1–7)

Acts 6:1–7 records an account of internal division in the early church. The Greek-speaking Hellenists[1] believed their widows were being treated unfairly by the local Hebrews in the church. How do the apostles handle this potentially divisive situation?

2. Stephen Is Seized (6:8–7:53)

In Stephen's speech, he takes the time to walk eloquently through salvation history. He begins with Abraham and God's promises to him (7:2–8). Read Genesis 12:1–3. What are these promises? Considering Acts 3:25–26, how were they fulfilled through Jesus?

Stephen tells Israel's history from Abraham, through slavery in Egypt, to Moses (Acts 7:9–19). Read Acts 7:20–43. Considering verses 27, 35, and 39, what point is Stephen making about Moses and his relationship to Israel? How is this relevant to the Jewish leaders' current opposition to Jesus? Considering verse 42, how did God respond to those who rejected Moses?

Stephen gives an overview of the presence of God throughout Israel's salvation history (7:42–50). He moves from God's presence in the tabernacle, to the temple, to a quote from Isaiah 66:1–2. What is his point about God's presence? Remembering the accusations against Stephen in Acts 6:13–14, what indictment against the Jewish leaders is he implying?

Finally, Stephen concludes with a direct, sharp attack on the religious leaders (Acts 7:51–53). What does he accuse them of? How does Stephen's speech up to this point condemn the leaders?

3. The Martyrdom of Stephen (7:54–60)

Acts 7 ends with the stoning of Stephen and the introduction of Saul (7:54–60). At the beginning of this episode, (6:10), Stephen's accusers could not withstand the wisdom of the Spirit, so they falsely accused him. Through it all, how would you characterize Stephen's response to this injustice?

Stephen prayed for two things as he died. The first ("Lord Jesus, receive my spirit"; Acts 7:59) recalls Jesus' dying words from the cross (Luke 23:46), and the second ("Lord, do not hold this sin against them") recalls Jesus' earlier prayer for the forgiveness of those responsible for his death (Luke 23:34). How could Stephen ask God not to "hold this sin against them" (Acts 7:60)?

Read through the following three sections on *Gospel Glimpses, Whole-Bible Connections*, and *Theological Soundings*. Then take time to consider the *Personal Implications* these sections may have for you.

Gospel Glimpses

THE GRACE OF GOD TO THOSE WHO OPPOSE JESUS. The "priests" mentioned in Acts 6:7 are significant. It was this very group that up to this point had been the most vehemently opposed to the gospel. This reminds us of the scope of the gospel: it is to be preached to everyone, even those who hate Christians and desire their deaths. Priests and Pharisees[2] were a major group of antagonists during the life and ministry of Jesus. They instigated and influenced his death, and Jesus also uttered his strongest words against religious leaders. Their faith in Christ, later in Acts, is a reflection of the power of the gospel and the grace of God to those who opposed Jesus.

SELFLESS LOVE MOTIVATED BY THE GOSPEL. The gospel has so permeated Stephen's life that, when faced with an unjust death at the hands of an angry mob, his dying breath is spent pleading with God to forgive them (Acts 7:60). His model here is Jesus, who prayed for the forgiveness of his persecutors, even as they crucified him (Luke 23:34, 46). It is difficult to imagine a more dramatic example of loving one's enemies (Luke 6:27–28). Stephen's selfless love is motivated by the gospel. Christ died for Stephen while Stephen was yet a sinner, showering him with undeserved grace. As a response to this grace, Stephen extends a reflection of that grace to his persecutors. The grace of God motivates mercy in his followers. Stephen's death makes an impression on Saul, who alludes to it later after his conversion (Acts 22:20). The persecutor of the church would soon become its most famous advocate, joining Stephen in experiencing the abundant grace of God and responding with grace to all around him.

Whole-Bible Connections

CHRIST AND THE OLD TESTAMENT. In response to the charge in Acts 6:13 that Jesus and his followers oppose the Mosaic law and aim both to abolish it and to destroy the temple, Stephen retells the story of Israel to reveal Jesus as the fulfillment of God's dealings with Israel throughout history (just as Jesus himself claimed to be in Matt. 5:17). In Stephen's speech, God's redemptive plan starts with his promises to the patriarchs in Genesis to give an inheritance to the offspring of Abraham. Throughout Israel's circuitous history of slavery in Egypt, the exodus, settling in the Promised Land, and the construction of the temple under Solomon, God was graciously orchestrating events to lead to the coming of the promised offspring, the Righteous One, Jesus. Christianity is not something new that breaks away from the Old Testament. Luke continually defends this claim in Acts. Christ's incarnation, ministry, death, and resurrection are the true fulfillment of the Old Testament promises of God. Jesus did not overrule and obliterate the revelation of God that had been entrusted to the Jews; he embodied and fulfilled it. The first Christians insist that the God who raised Jesus is the same God who acted powerfully and faithfully throughout the Old Testament—indeed, the Christian gospel depends on this identification. God's loving commitment to Israel across time and space provides a thickness to the good news in Acts, as people are not being urged to join a new fad but are offered the undeserved gift of being grafted into God's centuries-long redemptive program by the blood of Christ (Rom. 11:17–24; Eph. 2:12–13).

JESUS AND MOSES. For Jews, Moses was seen as the prophet on whom their religious traditions hinged. The indictment that the Jewish authorities brought against Stephen in Acts 6 and 7 is not a matter of mere abstract theological debate or nuance, because the law of Moses shaped nearly everything the Jews in Jesus' day thought about themselves and God. In Deuteronomy 18:15–18 Moses spoke of the promised Messiah as one who would be "a prophet like me." The claim of the New Testament is that Jesus came not to nullify the words of Moses but rather to fulfill them. As Moses led Israel toward the Promised Land and their redemption, so does Jesus for God's people today. The land promised to Christians is heaven.

THE PROPHETS. As Stephen retells the story of Israel, he highlights the fact that God's chosen prophets—Abraham, Joseph, Moses, and David—have always been mistreated by their own people. Stephen concludes his speech with a direct attack on the Jewish authorities (Acts 7:51–53), arguing that they, like the Jewish leaders of old, have persecuted and rejected God's prophets. Jesus stands as the last in the long line of God's prophets, and he too was persecuted by his own, even to the point of death. The great difference between the prophets of old and Jesus is that they spoke of the Righteous One to come, whereas Jesus *is* that Righteous One. It was through the persecution and death of the Righteous One that our sin was removed and we can now share in his righteousness, as in fact we do (2 Cor. 5:21).

GOD'S DWELLING AMONG HIS PEOPLE. Stephen turns to the golden era of Israel, the days of David and Solomon, to make the point that the Jews have mistakenly associated God's presence only with the temple. He shows that even in the Old Testament, by God's own words, he is not limited to a structure made with human hands (Acts 7:48–50). God is near to all who call on him (Ps. 145:18), and he has drawn near to us most fully in Jesus Christ, the Righteous One. In the Old Testament, God made his dwelling among the Jews in the form of the tabernacle, a temporary tent that allowed Israel to say, "The glory of God is with us" (Ex. 40:34–35). In the incarnation of Christ, God came to dwell among us, taking on flesh so that we may truly call him Immanuel, God with us (John 1:14; Matt. 1:23).

> **Theological Soundings**

SON OF MAN. In Acts 7:55–56, Stephen has a vision of the exalted Christ and calls him "the Son of Man." This is the title Jesus uses more than any other to refer to himself (e.g., Matt. 8:20; 11:19; 16:13). This phrase is most significant, not as a declaration of incarnate humanness, but in relation to the figure in Daniel 7:13–14 who receives supreme authority and an everlasting kingdom from God (compare Matt. 26:64; Mark 14:62).

THE WORK OF THE SPIRIT. The Holy Spirit of God, in his presence and fullness, is given credit for the resolution of the conflict between the Hebrews and the Hellenists in Acts 6. Additionally, the Spirit is given credit for Stephen's peace during his martyrdom in Acts 7. The Spirit is the third person of the Trinity, who is at work in applying the finished work of Christ in the lives of God's people. He is the one who enables the apostles to accomplish all their kingdom-advancing work, and he is the one who again and again enables and empowers Jesus' disciples down through the ages. Likewise, he is the one who enables and empowers us today to be his witnesses and his disciples, producing in us the "fruit of the Spirit" (Gal. 5:22–23).

THE PRESENCE OF GOD. Christians from the start have thought and spoken of God as "omnipresent." God is present everywhere with his whole being. Jeremiah 23:23–24, for example, states, "Am I a God at hand, declares the LORD, and not a God far away? Can a man hide himself in secret places so that I cannot see him? declares the LORD. Do I not fill heaven and earth?" One cannot run or hide from the presence of God. However, Scripture also describes the covenant presence of God as special. In Acts 7:33 and 7:44–50, Stephen mentions the uniqueness of God's presence with and for his people. In Jesus, the personal presence of God has been made available to all. Jesus is the covenant presence of God fully realized.

Personal Implications

Take time to reflect on the implications of Acts 6–7 for your own life today. Consider what you have learned that might lead you to praise God, repent of sin, and trust in his gracious promises. Make notes below on the personal implications for your walk with the Lord of the (1) *Gospel Glimpses*, (2) *Whole-Bible Connections*, (3) *Theological Soundings*, and (4) this passage as a whole.

1. Gospel Glimpses

2. Whole-Bible Connections

3. Theological Soundings

4. Acts 6:1–7:60

As You Finish This Unit . . .

Take a moment now to ask for the Lord's blessing and help as you continue in this study of Acts. Take a moment also to look back through this unit of study, to reflect on some key things that the Lord may be teaching you—and perhaps to highlight and underline these things to review again in the future

Definitions

[1] **Hellenists** – Jews who immigrated into Jerusalem from other parts of the Roman empire, for whom Greek was their first and perhaps only language. As such, when wives lost their husbands they would likely not have had a kinship network close at hand to care for them (and thus the "complaint"; Acts 6:1).

[2] **Pharisees** – A popular religious/political party in NT times characterized by strict adherence to the law of Moses and also to extrabiblical Jewish traditions. The Pharisees were frequently criticized by Jesus for their legalistic and hypocritical practices. The apostle Paul was a zealous Pharisee prior to his conversion.

WEEK 6: SAUL

Acts 8:1–9:31

▲

Stephen's murder kicks off a serious persecution led by Saul, and the young Christian community is scattered away from Jerusalem throughout the surrounding areas of Judea and Samaria. In the next four chapters (8–11), Acts moves from persecution to the gospel spreading across borders and boundaries: first to the Samaritans, then to the Gentiles. God's purposes continue to work through and overcome every obstacle, as what is intended to crush the movement becomes fuel for the gospel's advance.

In Acts 8:1–9:31 the church faces its fiercest opposition yet in the persecution led by Saul, but this violence actually serves to advance God's work and spread the gospel out from Jerusalem.

> ## Reflection and Discussion

Read the entire text for this week's study, Acts 8:1–9:31. Then review the following questions concerning this section of Acts and write your notes on them. (For further background, see the *ESV Study Bible*, pages 2096–2101, or visit esv.org.)

1. The Gospel Goes to Samaria (8:1–25)

Samaritans, though technically "half" Jewish, were considered non-Jewish, even of lower status than Gentiles, by the Jews of the first century. The Samaritans were not thought by Jews to have any part in the promises of God to his people. In Acts 8:4–25, the gospel reaches Samaria, and thus the first cross-cultural barrier is breached. To what degree is this a fulfillment of Jesus' words in Acts 1:8?

The story of Simon the magician in Acts 8:9–25 illustrates well the teachings of Acts on receiving the Holy Spirit. God is the sovereign giver of the Spirit. There are no mechanisms, techniques, or formulas that one can muster up to manipulate God's activity. Compare Peter's response to Simon in Acts 8:20 in light of what we read in Acts 2:38, 10:45, and 11:17. How is the Holy Spirit described?

2. The Conversion of Saul (9:1–31)

In Acts 9:1–9, Saul learns firsthand how closely Jesus identifies with his church, here described as "the Way." In persecuting those of the Way, Saul is persecuting Christ himself. In response to his question, "Who are you?" Saul would surely prefer any response to the one he receives: "I am Jesus, *whom you are persecuting.*" What do Jesus' words in verse 4 imply about his relationship with the church?

Reread Gamaliel's words in Acts 5:38–39. How is Saul fulfilling Gamaliel's prudent words? In opposing God's people, whom is Saul also opposing?

God can and will reach to his farthest-out enemies. He will defeat the uttermost human rebellion, but in doing so he does not crush rebels but loves and converts them into chosen instruments of the good news (9:15). How is the conversion[1] of Saul a picture of God's radical grace? How does it give you confidence and hope in the power and work of the gospel?

Paul was intent on preaching Christ after his conversion (Acts 9:20–22, 26–30). Twice (9:27, 28) we read that Paul "preached boldly" (one word in Greek). That word occurs only nine times in the New Testament, with seven times in Acts and the other two in Paul's letters as he recalls the manner in which he preached (Eph. 6:20; 1 Thess. 2:2). Read Acts 9:22, 29–30. What are the responses to Paul's preaching?

Read through the following three sections on *Gospel Glimpses*, *Whole-Bible Connections*, and *Theological Soundings*. Then take time to consider the *Personal Implications* these sections may have for you.

Gospel Glimpses

THE GOSPEL IN ISAIAH 53. It is no accident that the Ethiopian eunuch is reading from Isaiah 53 in Acts 8:32–33. It is clear that the Holy Spirit has led him there, and that the Lord has led Philip to this man who is in need of explanation. Isaiah 53 would have been a great place to begin to explain how the Messiah, the "man of sorrows" (Isa. 53:3), would be the one "stricken," "smitten," and "afflicted" by God (Isa. 53:4), the one who "was pierced for our transgressions" and "crushed for our iniquities" (Isa. 53:5). He willingly took this injustice for our sake, because we all "like sheep have gone astray; we have turned—every one—to his own way" (Isa. 53:6), and Jesus, the suffering Messiah, "bore the sin of many, and makes intercession for the transgressors" (Isa. 53:12).

GRACE AT OUR WORST. In the conversion of Saul (Acts 9:1–19), we receive a glimpse of the radical grace that God will show to and through Saul of Tarsus: God does not leave behind even one who supervises the murder of innocent Christians. Such behavior by the man who would become the "apostle to the Gentiles" (Rom. 11:13), through Christ, offers hope to sinners who feel unforgivable; we should never write off either ourselves or others as beyond redemption. Saul was at his worst, overseeing the murder of men and women in the church, with no sign of repentance,[2] when Jesus met him on the Damascus road. In Saul, we see a rebel against God, who committed cosmic treason and was an enemy of God. He is reconciled to God through Jesus and now calls himself God's ambassador, through whom God makes his appeal to the entire world (2 Cor. 5:20).

Whole-Bible Connections

GOD'S HEART FOR THE AFFLICTED. In the midst of intense persecution, here in Acts 8:4–25 we see how God cares for the suffering. God's heart has always been with the afflicted. When Israel was enslaved in Egypt, God heard their cries, saw their affliction, and knew their suffering (Ex. 3:7). He was involved. After redeeming Israel from Egypt, he gave them the law, replete with instructions to protect the poor, the outsiders, orphans, and widows (Deut. 10:18–19; 15:7–11). God's suffering servants have always been sinners as well. God's people often went after idols, forsaking him and enslaving themselves to pagan gods that could not deliver them (Isa. 45:20; Jer. 2:13). Christ is the obedient Servant who suffered without any sin. He walked in obedience to the Father but still suffered greatly, allowing him to identify both with the Father in his perfection and with us in our weakness and pain (Heb. 4:15). This qualifies Jesus to be the unique mediator between God and humanity.

UNITY AND FELLOWSHIP OF BELIEVERS. The Samaritans were considered racial "half-breeds." Here in Acts 8:14–17, it appears that God withholds the full ministry of Spirit until the apostles arrive in order to draw a connection between the Jerusalem church and the Samaritans. Otherwise, the Samaritans may have assumed autonomy from Jerusalem, or Jerusalem may not have accepted them as full brothers and sisters in the family of God. The important point is that even the Samaritans, whom the Jews usually avoided, were now filled with the Spirit, which testified that they were to be included in the church as full members of this expanding family of God. Again, the unity and fellowship of believers as the people of God is highlighted in Acts.

Theological Soundings

DEITY OF CHRIST. In Acts 9:20, Jesus is called "the Son of God." One layer of meaning here may highlight the deity of Christ. Jesus is "the Son of God," not only in that he is the one called by God to rule the earth as God's representative, but also in that he *is* God. The New Testament teaches that Jesus is included in the divine identity (1 Cor. 8:6; Rom. 9:5; Col. 1:15–20; Heb. 1:3). While there are distinctions of persons within the one Godhead, Jesus Christ is as truly God as are God the Father and God the Holy Spirit.

REDEMPTION. In this passage we see God redeeming all kinds of people: Samaritans, an Ethiopian, and Saul. Throughout Scripture, redemption is the work of God to deliver his people from the slavery of sin and from its penalty of death. In Genesis 3 God set in motion his plan to save his people from sin and judgment and set free the entire creation from its subjugation to sin and the curse. How? By sending his Son as a man who would bear the penalty for our sin and die in our place (1 Cor. 15:3). This is the message of the gospel. Redemption is a gift, freely given though undeserved, whereby we are rescued and delivered from sin and restored to a right relationship with God.

Personal Implications

Take time to reflect on the implications of Acts 8:1–9:31 for your own life today. Consider what you have learned that might lead you to praise God, repent of sin, and trust in his gracious promises. Make notes below on the personal implications for your walk with the Lord of the (1) *Gospel Glimpses*, (2) *Whole-Bible Connections*, (3) *Theological Soundings*, and (4) this passage as a whole.

1. Gospel Glimpses

2. Whole-Bible Connections

3. Theological Soundings

4. Acts 8:1–9:31

As You Finish This Unit . . .

Take a moment now to ask for the Lord's blessing and help as you continue in this study of Acts. Take a moment also to look back through this unit of study, to reflect on some key things that the Lord may be teaching you—and perhaps to highlight and underline these things to review again in the future.

Definitions

[1] **Conversion** – The process of turning away from sin, accepting the truth of the gospel of Jesus Christ, and submitting to him.

[2] **Repentance** – A complete change of heart and mind regarding one's overall attitude toward God and one's individual actions. True regeneration, expressed in conversion, is always accompanied by repentance.

Week 7: The Gospel to the Gentiles

Acts 9:32–12:25

▲

The previous section of Acts recorded the conversion of the gospel's fiercest opponent, Saul, into its greatest missionary. Now the significant barrier between Jews and Gentiles is overcome as God leads Peter to bring the gospel to the Gentiles, and the Jewish Christians begin to realize that God is offering salvation to *all* people through the work of Jesus. God can make all things clean, and from here on in Acts we begin to see that the gospel overcomes all obstacles, whether ethnic, cultural, religious, or political.

The Big Picture

In Acts 9:32–12:25 we see the outpouring of the Holy Spirit on the Gentiles, dramatically demonstrating that the barrier between Jews and Gentiles is being demolished and salvation is now streaming out to all nations.

Reflection and Discussion

Read through the complete passage for this study, Acts 9:32–12:25. Then review the questions below and record your notes and reflections on this section of Acts. (For further background, see the *ESV Study Bible*, pages 2102–2108, or visit esv.org.)

In Acts 9:32–35, when Peter encounters Aeneas, who was paralyzed, Peter says "Jesus Christ heals you" (9:34). Peter understands that Jesus is working to build his church. As is often the case in Acts, miracles such as this healing lead to the advancement of the gospel. The news spreads beyond the town of Lydda to the whole coastal plain of Sharon, and all the residents "turned to the Lord" (9:35). How is this similar to the healing of the lame man and the preaching of the gospel in Acts 3?

In 10:9–16 Peter is given a strange and disturbing vision. A "great sheet" descends on earth from heaven. In it are all kinds of animals, reptiles, and birds. Then a voice tells Peter to "kill and eat." What is Peter's initial response (10:14)? What reason does he give for his response?

The voice says, "What God has made clean, do not call common" (10:15). Then, the whole vision is repeated three times. Peter does not initially understand the meaning of the vision (v. 17), but the Holy Spirit leads him to three Gentiles (vv. 17–18). Later, Peter puts all the pieces together (v. 28). What connection is God making for Peter between the unclean[1] animals in the vision and Cornelius and his household?

In the story of Peter and Cornelius (Acts 10:1–48), we see one of the most revolutionary features of the good news: its demolition of the barrier between Jews and Gentiles. The story of the conversion of Cornelius is the longest narrative in the book of Acts. It is a very significant moment in the gospel's advance, as God is showing that the gospel is for all people, not just the Jews. How is this part of the continued fulfillment of Jesus' words in Acts 1:8?

The Jewish believers with Peter are shocked that the Holy Spirit is poured out even on the Gentiles (Acts 10:45). They probably thought that Gentiles should become Jewish proselytes first, but they knew the Holy Spirit had come to the Gentiles when they heard them speaking in tongues and praising God (v. 46). Because these Gentiles had received the Holy Spirit, there was nothing to prevent them from being baptized as Christians. Verse 47 quotes the reaction of the Jewish believers: They "have received the Holy Spirit just as we have." The reference to Acts 2 is obvious. The same Holy Spirit who had been poured out on Jews had also been poured out on Gentiles. God can make all things clean. The conclusion embraced by Peter and by the Jerusalem church was that these Gentiles were fellow believers. Repentance and salvation had been granted even to those who had not come under the Mosaic covenant. How does the conclusion embraced by Peter (Acts 10:47–48; 11:15–17) and the Jerusalem church (Acts 11:18) reveal that these Gentiles were fellow believers?

In Acts 11:1–18, Peter recounts to the apostles and the church in Jerusalem the news of Cornelius's conversion and the Gentiles' reception of the Holy Spirit. In 11:2–3 Peter receives some harsh criticism from the "circumcision party." Note, however, the change of attitude from 11:2–3 to 11:18. Like Peter before, the Jewish Christians in Jerusalem were thinking that God still wanted separation between Jews and Gentiles. Looking at verses 4–17, what things changed their understanding?

Herod's role is brief. Having executed James, he plans to put Peter to a similar end, before God intervenes and foils his plot (Acts 12:6–19). Here is a blatant opponent to the work of God, motivated not as Saul was by religious zeal, but by the desire for acclaim (v. 3). This idolatrous desire proves to be Herod's undoing. Herod accepts the praises of the crowd, attributing to him divine eloquence. How does Herod's response compare with Peter's swift denial when Cornelius seeks to worship him (10:26) and Paul's vehement protests when the people of Lystra mistake him for the god Hermes (14:11–15)?

Read through the following three sections on *Gospel Glimpses*, *Whole-Bible Connections*, and *Theological Soundings*. Then take time to consider the *Personal Implications* these sections may have for you.

Gospel Glimpses

PURE IN CHRIST. Christians can be tempted to doubt God's salvation, as Satan reminds us of the unclean blemish of sin in our lives. Satan will attack us with feelings of guilt and shame. Peter's vision (Acts 10:9–16), however, reminds us that what God has called clean, we have no right to call unclean (v. 15). If we have put our faith in Christ, God sees us as pure, and how God sees things is how they truly are. There is no condemnation for those in Christ (Rom. 8:1), for he has removed our sins as far as the east is from the west (Ps. 103:12); he has made our scarlet sins as white as snow (Isa. 1:18). We no longer regard ourselves or others according to what we can see, as we used to, and as we once wrongly regarded Christ himself. Instead we regard ourselves and others according to the Spirit, through whom God has made us clean, pure, and whole (2 Cor. 5:16).

"ALL." In Peter's gospel presentation to Cornelius and his household in Acts 10:34–43, one of the repeated words is "all." Over and over again, Peter uses the inclusive language of "all" to emphasize that Jesus Christ is "Lord of all" (v. 36), and "truly, God shows no partiality" (v. 34). What Peter tells Cornelius's household he tells us as well: that God shows no partiality, but freely receives all who believe in his Son, Jesus Christ. Both Jew and Gentile are given one path to forgiveness (15:11). Before the cross of Christ, all distinctions fall away. The cross is the great equalizer: at the foot of the cross, we are all humbled as we grasp the magnitude of our sin and guilt; yet at the cross, the offer of forgiveness is made without bias or favoritism. Because Jesus is Lord of all (10:36), his gospel is available to all.

Whole-Bible Connections

PURITY LAWS. The ritual food purity laws recorded in Leviticus 11 and Deuteronomy 14 set Israel apart from other nations as God's holy people and expressed their devotion to the Lord. By downplaying the purity laws, Peter's vision in Acts 10:9–16 represents a significant paradigm shift in the early church's understanding of the gospel. Up to this time, individual Gentiles had been saved by becoming a part of the people of God represented by the nation of Israel (e.g., Ruth and Rahab). Now God is communicating that the gospel does not require Gentiles to become a part of Israel's national identity. God's grace is now going out to the nations.

LIGHT TO THE NATIONS. For Jewish Christians, the inclusion of the Gentiles into the people of God would have felt like an unbelievable paradigm shift. In Acts 11:1–18, the power of the gospel is seen in both the inclusion of the Gentiles into the people of God and in the church's acceptance of them. There were many different outlooks on Gentiles among Jews during this time, but one cannot argue from the Old Testament that Gentiles (such as Cornelius, the Ethiopian eunuch, or the Roman centurion in Luke 7:1–10) are ignored or excluded by God. God had chosen Israel to be a people set apart, but they were meant to be a blessing to the nations (Gen. 12:3; 22:16–18; Isa. 42:6; 49:6). Associating with Gentiles was not "unlawful" (Acts 10:28) in terms of violating Old Testament commands but in the sense of not following the later customs of strict Jewish traditions about uncleanness. The Jewish traditions of purity made it virtually impossible for Jews to associate with Gentiles without becoming ritually unclean. Now Peter is shown that the same God who chose Israel is doing a new thing, bringing Israel's vocation—to be a "light to the nations"—to its fullness by embracing the Gentiles through the perfect Israelite: Jesus, the Light of the world.

Theological Soundings

GOSPEL PRESENTATION. In his gospel presentation in Acts 10:34–43, Peter does not quote the Old Testament, but his message remains consistent: Jesus lived, died, and was raised; he has been appointed by God as judge of the living and the dead; and everyone is called to repent and believe, to receive forgiveness of sins through the name of Jesus. This is the culmination of God's redemptive plan.

VISIONS. The expression "the heavens opened" (Acts 10:11) would have reminded readers of other significant communications from God, such as the dove and the voice at the baptism of Jesus (Luke 3:21) and, in this same book of Acts, Stephen's vision of the exalted Christ just before his martyrdom (Acts 7:56). In sending Peter this vision, God is demonstrating the supreme importance of the message that he is able to make anyone clean, and that he has chosen to bring cleansing and salvation through Christ to all the nations.

Personal Implications

Take time to reflect on the implications of Acts 9:32–12:25 for your own life today. Consider what you have learned that might lead you to praise God, repent of sin, and trust in his gracious promises. Make notes below on the personal implications for your walk with the Lord of the (1) *Gospel Glimpses*, (2) *Whole-Bible Connections*, (3) *Theological Soundings*, and (4) this passage as a whole.

1. Gospel Glimpses

2. Whole-Bible Connections

3. Theological Soundings

4. Acts 9:32–12:25

> ### As You Finish This Unit . . .

Take a moment now to ask for the Lord's blessing and help as you continue in this study of Acts. Take a moment also to look back through this unit of study, to reflect on some key things that the Lord may be teaching you—and perhaps to highlight and underline these things to review again in the future.

Definitions

[1] **Clean/unclean** – The ceremonial, spiritual, or moral state of a person or object, affected by a variety of factors. The terms are primarily related to the concept of holiness and have little to do with actual physical cleanliness. The Mosaic law declared certain foods and animals unclean, and a person became unclean if he or she came in contact with certain substances or objects, such as a dead body. Jesus declared all foods clean (Mark 7:19), and Peter's vision in Acts 10 shows that no person is ceremonially unclean simply because he or she is a Gentile.

WEEK 8: PAUL AND BARNABAS ARE SENT

Acts 13:1–14:28

▲

The Place of the Passage

Through Peter's vision and the outpouring of the Holy Spirit on Cornelius's family in the previous section of Acts, God powerfully demonstrated that the gospel is going to the Gentiles. Now, Paul and Barnabas are sent out to preach, and we see the beginnings of the missionary movement that will take the gospel out from the Jewish homeland and into Asia Minor. Chapters 13 and 14 record Paul's "first missionary journey." A new recurring theme is introduced here as we repeatedly see the Jews rejecting the gospel while the Gentiles embrace it.

The Big Picture

Commissioned by the Antioch church, Paul and Barnabas set off on their first missionary journey to bring the gospel to the Gentiles in Acts 13–14.

Reflection and Discussion

Read through the complete passage for this study, Acts 13:1–14:28. Then review the questions below concerning this section of Acts and write your notes on them. (For further background, see the *ESV Study Bible*, pages 2109–2114, or visit esv.org.)

In Acts 13:3–4, Saul and Barnabas are sent out by the Holy Spirit. (Now that he is working in Gentile territory, the Hebrew "Saul" becomes known by his Roman name, "Paul"; 13:9) Where do Paul and Barnabas start preaching first when they arrive in Cyprus (13:5), in Antioch of Pisidia (v. 14), and in Iconium (14:1)? Considering Acts 3:25–26 and 13:46, why is this pattern noteworthy? In what way is it a partial fulfillment of Jesus' words in Acts 1:8?

In 13:10–11, Paul delivers a seemingly harsh pronouncement on the magician Elymas. One can hear an echo of God's mercy in Paul's own life, when he himself was sternly rebuked for opposing Christ and was struck with blindness for a time. What does the text say was the result of Paul's rebuke (13:11–12)?

In Acts 13:14, Paul and Barnabas preach the gospel. What are the core elements of the gospel found in verses 28, 30, 31, 34, and 38?

In Acts 13:45–52, Jewish opposition to the gospel once again begins to rise. Paul writes in 1 Corinthians 1:22–23 that "Jews demand signs and Greeks seek wisdom, but we preach Christ crucified, a stumbling block to Jews and folly to Gentiles." The "stumbling block to Jews" of Christ crucified has been a common theme through Acts so far. What is the reason given for Jewish opposition in Acts 13:44–45? What happens when the Gentiles are offered the good news (vv. 48–49)?

God's grace begins to multiply and spread through the Gentiles in the region. What does the text give as the determining factor in who believed the gospel (Acts 13:48 and 14:27)? Read Ephesians 2:1–10. Where does Paul say that faith comes from?

Read through the following three sections on *Gospel Glimpses*, *Whole-Bible Connections*, and *Theological Soundings*. Then take time to consider the *Personal Implications* these sections may have for you.

Gospel Glimpses

LAW AND GOSPEL. Preaching in Antioch of Pisidia, Paul declares that with the coming of Christ, forgiveness[1] of sins is now available (Acts 13:38–39). Faith in Christ brings a freedom that the law[2] of Moses could not achieve. The law of Moses gave temporary provision for sin by instituting priests to mediate between God and his people, but the law could not lead to eternal and ultimate forgiveness. The law serves only to heighten our understanding of our own sin, not to lessen it (Rom. 7:7–12). Through Christ we can avail ourselves of a power that the law never had. The law hung over us as a ministry of death, threatening to kill us for our sins; the Spirit of Christ delivers us from the bondage of sin, guilt, and death into new life (2 Cor. 3:6–7). What the law was powerless to do, because it was weakened by the flesh, God did by sending his own Son in the likeness of sinful flesh to be a sin offering (Rom 8:3). God's grace is overflowing and abundant (Rom. 5:15, 17; 6:1; 2 Cor. 4:15; 8:9; 9:8, 14). It is also powerful: grace motivates changed lives, as Paul writes: "The love of Christ controls us!" (2 Cor. 5:14). The law threatens and demands, but does not motivate. This is not to discount the value of the law. The law of God is "perfect . . . true, and righteous altogether" (Ps. 19:7–9) and "holy and righteous and good" (Rom. 7:12), but it does not enable people to do what it demands. Paul writes, "If a law had been given that could give life, then righteousness would indeed be by the law" (Gal. 3:21). Law does not empower us to do what it mandates—but grace does (Matt. 10:8; Rom. 2:4; Rom. 6:14; Titus 2:11–12).

Whole-Bible Connections

SENT ONE. In Acts 14:4, 14 the term "apostles" is used of Paul and Barnabas, neither of whom are in the list of "the twelve" (Matt. 10:1–4; 26:14). So this is a more extended use of the term than just "the twelve." Even if Paul views himself as an apostle based on Jesus speaking directly to him and commissioning him, this would not be true for Barnabas. Paul seems to include Barnabas as well in his analysis of apostleship in 1 Corinthians 9:1–6 (see also 2 Cor. 8:23, where the word "messenger" is the same Greek word *apostoloi*; and see Phil. 2:25, where Epaphroditus is also called a "messenger," using this same word).

PAUL'S HEART FOR THE GENTILES. The reference in Acts 13:46–47 to Isaiah 49:6 shows that the inclusion of the Gentiles was God's plan all along. Another reason the gospel is indeed good news is that it extends God's people from being ethnic in origin (Israel) to a people based completely on faith in the crucified and resurrected Savior Jesus Christ. Paul's speech here (Acts 13:46–47) is similar to his longer, written version in Romans 15:14–21, where he demonstrates that the Gentiles were always part of God's plan of salvation. Acts 13:46–47 is perhaps where Paul officially turns toward the Gentiles, sparking his ambition to "preach the gospel, not where Christ has already been named" (Rom. 15:20). Romans ends with three verses that are about the gospel being made known to "all nations" (16:25–27).

Theological Soundings

GOD'S INITIATIVE. Repeatedly in Acts we see that God's grace plays the crucial role in the advance of the gospel, as even repentance and faith are gifts from God. When the Gentiles hear the gospel, "as many as were appointed to eternal life believed" (Acts 13:48). Faith in Christ comes as a result of God's gracious initiative, and even belief in the gospel is a gift of God's grace, as Paul and Barnabas acknowledge when they revel in the fact that God "had opened a door of faith to the Gentiles" (Acts 14:27).

COMMON GRACE. Although God chose the Jews to be the special recipients of his revelation, he did not leave the rest of the world "without witness" (Acts 14:17). Not only Scripture but all of creation speaks of God (Psalm 19). He alone is the giver of all good gifts and the source of all blessing (James 1:17). However, we are prone to attribute the glory of God to lesser things, and this leads to idolatry. This is what we see here at Lystra: in light of the power of God that Paul displayed, the people of Lystra begin to offer sacrifices to Paul and Barnabas. They cannot help but worship, but their worship finds the wrong object.

Personal Implications

Take time to reflect on the implications of Acts 13–14 for your own life today. Consider what you have learned that might lead you to praise God, repent of sin, and trust in his gracious promises. Make notes below on the personal implications for your walk with the Lord of the (1) *Gospel Glimpses*, (2) *Whole-Bible Connections*, (3) *Theological Soundings*, and (4) this passage as a whole.

1. Gospel Glimpses

2. Whole-Bible Connections

3. Theological Soundings

4. Acts 13:1–14:28

As You Finish This Unit . . .

Take a moment now to ask for the Lord's blessing and help as you continue in this study of Acts. Take a moment also to look back through this unit of study, to reflect on some key things that the Lord may be teaching you—and perhaps to highlight and underline these things to review again in the future.

Definitions

[1] **Forgiveness** – Release from guilt and the reestablishment of relationship. Forgiveness can be granted by God to human beings (Luke 24:47; 1 John 1:9) and by human beings to those who have wronged them (Matt. 18:21–22; Col. 3:13).

[2] **Law** – When spelled with an initial capital letter, "Law" refers to the first five books of the Bible (the Pentateuch). The Law contains numerous commands of God to his people, including the Ten Commandments and instructions regarding worship, sacrifice, and life in Israel. The NT often uses "the law" (lower case) to refer to the entire body of precepts set forth in the books of the Law.

Week 9: The Jerusalem Council

Acts 15:1–35

The Place of the Passage

After Paul and Barnabas complete their first missionary journey, the gospel has begun to take greater root among the Gentiles, but a religious faction arises to teach that Gentile Christians must be circumcised[1] and must follow the law of Moses to be saved. In Acts 15, the church convenes a major assembly, known as the "Jerusalem council," to discuss conditions for Gentile membership in the church and what is necessary for salvation.

The Big Picture

In Acts 15:1–35, the Jerusalem council is convened to decide whether non-Jewish believers must submit to all the requirements of the law of Moses, and especially circumcision, in order to be accepted as brothers and sisters in Christ.

Reflection and Discussion

Read through the complete passage for this study, Acts 15:1–35. Then review the questions below concerning this section of Acts and write your notes on them. (For further background, see the *ESV Study Bible*, pages 2114–2117, or visit esv.org.)

Acts 15 opens up with a debate. Should Gentile Christians be circumcised? A small group of believers who "belonged to the party of the Pharisees" (15:5) say that "it is necessary to circumcise them and to order them to keep the law of Moses." Read Genesis 17:9–14. For a faithful Jew, what did circumcision mean? What was its significance for being a member of the covenant people of God?

Read Paul's narrative in Galatians 2:1–21. How does this help you understand more fully the issues in Acts 15?

Up to this point in Acts we have seen how the inclusion of the Gentiles and the pouring out of the Holy Spirit upon them was an unexpected paradigm shift for many Jewish believers. In Acts 15:7–9, Peter refers to the outpouring of the gospel at the house of Cornelius in 10:34–43. Peter then refers to the manner in which the Gentiles received the Spirit. In 15:7–9, to what does Peter refer?

In Acts 15:9, Peter's reference to God having cleansed the Gentiles' hearts by faith may allude to the content of his vision prior to visiting Cornelius: "What God has made clean, do not call common" (10:15; 11:9). The faith of the Gentiles at Cornelius's house is only implicit in Acts 10–11, but Peter referred to it explicitly here: they were saved by faith in their hearts, not by circumcision in their flesh. How does the argument here recall points made in 11:15–17?

In Acts 15:10, Peter refers to the law as a "yoke . . . that neither our fathers nor we have been able to bear." The law informed God's followers how to walk in integrity with him, but it never provided the power to obey it; instead, it only revealed the inability of God's people to live up to God's perfect righteousness. Through its system of sacrifices, the people of Israel were to look forward to the sacrifice that was to come, the true spotless lamb that would take away their sins forever (John 1:29). Consider Matthew 11:28–30. Who is Peter echoing when he calls the law an unbearable yoke?

Peter concludes his speech in Acts 15:11. What does he say? How does this support the unity of the church that would include both Gentile and Jewish believers?

In Acts 15:13–21, James responds emphatically that the Gentiles do not need to be circumcised. In the letter sent to the Gentile churches (vv. 22–29), James writes, "it has seemed good to the Holy Spirit and to us to lay on you no greater burden than these requirements." What are these "requirements"?

How do the Gentile Christians respond to the letter from the Jerusalem council (Acts 15:31)?

Read through the following three sections on *Gospel Glimpses, Whole-Bible Connections*, and *Theological Soundings*. Then take time to consider the *Personal Implications* these sections may have for you.

Gospel Glimpses

GRACE ALONE. The doctrine of *sola gratia*, "grace alone," teaches that there is nothing anyone can do that can contribute or add to their salvation in Christ. Peter's point in Acts 15:11 is that all are saved only by the grace[2] of God through faith in Jesus Christ. The Bible makes this point again and again—that there is nothing that we can do to earn God's favor. Our will is not a deciding factor (Rom. 8:7–8), nor is our (fancied) goodness. Even our faith, which is a matter of receiving rather than doing in any active sense, is a gift from God (Rom. 12:3; Eph. 2:8). All of our salvation is an undeserved, gracious gift from God.

FREEDOM IN CHRIST. The law binds, but the grace of Jesus frees (Gal. 5:1). As long as we attempt to salve our conscience through acting right, we will find ourselves bound to the taskmasters of guilt and fear: have I done enough? Is God pleased with me now? True freedom from guilt comes only when we recognize the boundless and undeserved love that God has poured out on us through his Son. Jesus has done enough for God to be pleased with us. As Peter declared, "we will be saved through the grace of the Lord Jesus" (Acts 15:11).

Whole-Bible Connections

THE YOKE OF THE LAW. In the Bible, graceless religion is presented as an intolerable burden that only brings discouragement and despair. When Peter refers to the law as a "yoke" that no one is able to carry (Acts 15:10), he is echoing the words of Jesus (Matt. 11:28–30). God favors the weak and burdened, not the spiritually proud. Jesus invites all who are worn out and carrying heavy burdens. His harshest words were for the Pharisees, who he says "tie up heavy burdens, hard to bear, and lay them on people's shoulders" (Matt. 23:4). Jesus is rebuking those who misunderstand the law and use it not to lead people to God's mercy but instead to weigh people down with heavy labor and impossible expectations. Jesus contrasts his "yoke" with the yoke of the Pharisees, who heap burdens but do not lift a finger to help. Jesus is the opposite. Those who come to Jesus will find that his yoke is lighter, not because he demands less, but because Jesus bears the load for us. Jesus takes the yoke we are incapable of carrying, which Peter admits we are unable to bear, and then takes the whippings of the law for us at the cross. Our burden is light because Jesus takes the yoke that burdens us and does the work for us in our place.

THE WEAKER BROTHER. If circumcision is unnecessary for salvation, then why does the Jerusalem council give any restrictions at all? Here we see an example of the principle of respect for the "weaker" brother (see Romans 14; 1 Corinthians 8). The dietary restrictions imposed here were intended to show love and respect for the Jewish Christians. Because of their background, Jewish Christians would have struggled to share a meal with Gentiles who flaunted their traditional dietary customs. The Jerusalem council aims to avoid such potentially divisive offense by asking the Gentiles to accommodate their brothers and sisters. The response of the Gentile believers—joy—shows that they hardly view these requirements as burdensome. As Christ laid down his freedom for their sake, so they find joy in laying down their freedoms out of love for others.

Theological Soundings

SALVATION. Many Christians today understand "salvation" in the Bible in only an eternal sense. That is, "Because I am saved I go to heaven when I die." True! Praise God! But because of this, we may miss some of the meaning in our reading of Scripture. The Bible has a number of different uses and tenses of the words "salvation" and "save" (e.g., Num. 10:9; Mark 16:16; 1 Cor. 1:21; Eph. 2:5; Titus 3:5). God's plan is to save his people from their sins—and to bring them fully and finally to himself (Matt. 1:21; 2 Tim. 2:10). Christians experience salvation in this life in both a past and present sense, and we anticipate salvation in a future sense. We Christians have been saved from the penalty of our sins; we are currently being saved from the power of sin; and one day, when God's plan of salvation is completed and we are with Christ, we shall be like him, and we shall be saved from the presence of sin. This is God's plan of salvation.

GRACE IN PRACTICE. Timothy was not circumcised. Though circumcision was not one of the four regulations set in writing by the Jerusalem council, Paul will take Timothy with him in delivering those regulations. Paul therefore asks that Timothy be circumcised, not as a requirement for salvation or even an act of obedience to God, but to remove a significant barrier as both men minister to churches of Jewish and Gentile congregations. This was grace and love in practice to others on behalf of Paul and especially Timothy. Context and motivation are critical to Paul. He argues strongly *against* being circumcised if those arguing for circumcision believe that it is necessary in order to please God (Gal. 5:1–6); yet if the motivation is to remove barriers to people hearing about the grace of God, Paul will freely and gladly give up any number of cultural practices or preferences (1 Cor. 9:12–23).

JEWISH LAW. The Jewish law contained not only basic moral provisions but many aspects of a more "ceremonial" nature, such as circumcision, the kosher food laws, and many requirements involving external purity and various kinds of sacrifices and festivals. These laws presented a problem for Gentiles: to live by them would make it virtually impossible to continue in their Gentile communities. But according to the Old Testament, one had to be circumcised to belong to the people of God (Gen. 17:9–14), and it seemed to many of the Jewish Christians that the church should also require this of male believers. Paul addresses the issue of circumcision in Romans 2:25–29; 4:9–16; and Galatians 2:3–5; 5:2–12; 6:12–15.

Personal Implications

Take time to reflect on the implications of Acts 15:1–35 for your own life today. Consider what you have learned that might lead you to praise God, repent of sin, and trust in his gracious promises. Make notes below on the personal implications for your walk with the Lord of the (1) *Gospel Glimpses*, (2) *Whole-Bible Connections*, (3) *Theological Soundings*, and (4) this passage as a whole.

1. Gospel Glimpses

2. Whole-Bible Connections

3. Theological Soundings

4. Acts 15:1–35

As You Finish This Unit . . .

Take a moment now to ask for the Lord's blessing and help as you continue in this study of Acts. Take a moment also to look back through this unit of study, to reflect on some key things that the Lord may be teaching you—and perhaps to highlight and underline these things to review again in the future.

Definitions

[1] **Circumcision** – The ritual practice of removing the foreskin of an individual, which was commanded for all male Israelites in OT times as a sign of participation in the covenant God established with Abraham (Gen. 17:9–14).

[2] **Grace** – Unmerited favor, especially the free gift of salvation that God gives to believers through faith in Jesus Christ.

Week 10: Paul's Second and Third Missionary Journeys

Acts 15:36–21:16

The Place of the Passage

After the Jerusalem council's ruling that the Gentile Christians do not need to be circumcised for their salvation, Paul sets out on his second (Acts 15:36–18:22) and third (18:23–21:16) missionary journeys, taking Silas as his companion. As the gospel spreads throughout Asia Minor and the Roman world, God is at work through the ministry of Paul to bring all kinds of people to faith in Christ: from pagans[1] who have no knowledge of redemptive history, to people who, like Apollos, "knew of the baptism of John" but not of Jesus. We see numerous churches planted as the gospel message extends even further.

The Big Picture

In Acts 15:36–21:16, Paul and Silas follow the Lord's leading on their missionary journeys throughout Asia Minor and the Roman world.

> ## Reflection and Discussion

Read through the complete passage for this study, Acts 15:36–21:16. Then review the questions below concerning this section of Acts and write your notes on them. (For further background, see the *ESV Study Bible*, pages 2117–2131, or visit esv.org.)

1. Paul's Second Missionary Journey (Acts 15:36–18:22)

Acts 16:11–15 records the baptism of Lydia. The Lord is the one who graciously opens hearts to repent and believe the gospel. Consider 16:14. How does Luke emphasize that God is the active agent in bringing believers to faith in Christ? How is this fact also reflected in 18:27?

Acts 16:16–34 records Paul and Silas in prison. What is the jailer's question in 16:30? How do they answer him (16:31)? How does he respond (16:33–34)?

In Acts 17:1–15, the episodes in Thessalonica and nearby Berea offer vivid illustrations of nearly opposite reactions to the gospel. How does each city respond, respectively?

Paul's approach to the Greek elites of Athens is a contrast in preaching style to how he approaches the Jews in the synagogues, but it is the same gospel of the grace of God through Jesus Christ that he preaches to Jews and Greeks. Paul's outreach to the Gentiles, though it tends to stir up the Jews to jealousy, is simply a reflection of Jesus' gracious approach to outsiders.

Paul's speech at the Areopagus (Acts 17:22–34) offers an example of witnessing with relevance. He studies the culture to find the most relevant and engaging inroads for the gospel. Despite his passionate disdain for the idolatry of the city (v. 16), how does Paul begin his discourse (v. 22)? Knowing that his listeners are not familiar with the Old Testament Scriptures, whom does Paul quote (v. 28)?

Paul's understanding of the local culture, however, does not prevent him from confronting their misconceptions and denouncing their idols (Acts 17:29–30). The gospel has not changed, even though Paul's presentation of it begins in a much different manner than usual. Look at verses 30–31. What does Paul say God is commanding everyone to do (v. 30)? Why does he say they must do this (v. 31)? What assurance has God given (v. 31)?

Before Paul returned to Antioch to bring his second missionary journey to a close (Acts 18:18–22), he spends some time in Corinth (18:1–17). In 18:6 Paul seems frustrated. In verses 9–10 God speaks to Paul, encouraging him to remain in Corinth despite his frustrations, because God apparently has many people to bring to faith there. In the face of opposition, God steps in with faithful love to strengthen Paul's resolve. In 18:9–10, how does God promise his presence and protection?

---

2. Paul's Third Missionary Journey (Acts 18:23–21:16)

In Acts 19:1–7, we read that some Ephesians had become followers of John the Baptist and had received his baptism (see also 18:24–28, concerning the similar experience of Apollos). They knew that John pointed beyond himself to Jesus. They apparently knew of Jesus' life and ministry, and his death and resurrection, but *not* about the coming of the Spirit at Pentecost and its significance for the new era. These believers were in a salvation-history "time-warp," as if they were still in Acts 1, before the unfolding of redemptive history at Pentecost. The tongues of Acts 19:7 serve as the witness to the Ephesian believers themselves of the gift of the Spirit that transfers them as a group from the old era to the new one in which they should be living. How is this a continued fulfillment of Acts 1:8?

Read through the following three sections on *Gospel Glimpses*, *Whole-Bible Connections*, and *Theological Soundings*. Then take time to consider the *Personal Implications* these sections may have for you.

Gospel Glimpses

GOD'S RESCUE. Acts 16:25–34 is one of the most moving episodes in Acts. After Paul and Silas are savagely beaten and imprisoned for rescuing a girl from a dishonorable and probably oppressive occupation, we learn about the terror-ridden job of the Philippian jailer, one in which he faced death for any failure (see 12:19). He knows he has failed, he knows his fate, and he decides to take his own life. He has given up. But Paul enacts God's rescue of this man, reversing his world of failure by offering life in spite of failure. He and his household are saved through this grace, and Paul even offers to stay in prison in order to protect this man's life. Paul's example of selflessness leads to a stunned appeal for salvation and another example of God's grace poured out to suffering sinners.

THE WORD OF HIS GRACE. In Acts 20:24–38, Paul reminds the Ephesians of how God has worked in him to testify to the gospel of the grace of God (v. 24). He expresses confidence not in human ability but in "the word of his grace, which is able to build you up and to give you the inheritance among all those who are sanctified" (v. 32). Paul knows that the grace of God is more powerful than any laws, commands, or threats to motivate and build up his people, and he desires that they continue to live under the grace of God that has been poured out for them.

Whole-Bible Connections

JESUS IS LORD. In Thessalonica, the Christians are accused of "acting against the decrees of Caesar, saying there is another king, Jesus" (Acts 17:7). This is only half true. The lie is saying that Christians disobeyed Caesar. We know from historical sources that Christians, like Jews, were always very civil and law-abiding. The truth is that Christians of the first century refused to engage in acts of worshiping Caesar or acknowledging him as divine in any sense. In Roman society, such a refusal threatened social stability. Early Christians were not usually persecuted for worshiping Jesus, but for worshiping Jesus only. There is only one God, only one king. Jesus is Lord, not Caesar.

THE COMFORT OF GOD'S PRESENCE. It is God's presence ("I am with you"; Acts 18:10) that not only energizes believers but protects them from fear, anxiety, and doubt. God's presence casting out fear is a recurring theme in Scripture. Moses encouraged Joshua, "It is the LORD who goes before you. He will be with you; he will not leave you or forsake you. Do not fear or be dismayed" (Deut. 31:8; compare Josh. 1:9). The same thought and wording is used by David to his son Solomon in 1 Chronicles 28:29. Hezekiah uses the same language in 2 Chronicles 32:7–8 when faced with the invasion from the Assyrians. God offers comfort through his presence in the Prophets (see, e.g., Isa. 41:13–14 and Jer. 46:28), and the Psalms (e.g., Ps. 23:4). And Jesus promises his presence at the close of his last words of commission to the church: "Behold, I am with you always, to the end of the age" (Matt. 28:20).

Theological Soundings

FILLED WITH THE SPIRIT IN ACTS. In the second chapter of Acts, about 120 Jewish believers are filled with the Holy Spirit. In Acts 8, Samaritans—considered racial half-breeds by Jews—are filled with the Spirit after they believe the gospel preached by Philip. In Acts 10 and 11, Peter preaches to Gentiles, who believe and are filled with the Spirit. Here in 19:1–7, Paul meets some followers of John the Baptist who didn't know all that Jesus did and taught. So they believe and are filled with the Spirit. In this progression we see the ever-expanding scope of the gospel. God's mercy is poured out deep and wide. The Spirit's ministry is expansive, just as Jesus' was—including those who previously were excluded. The gospel-centered focus of Acts can be pictured by expanding concentric circles—the Holy Spirit brings Jesus' good news to a small group of disciples, to 120 Jews, to Samaritans, to Gentiles, and to the entire world.

ELDER. When individuals who believe the gospel and live Christ-centered lives come together, how do they worship corporately? One answer is that God has given human authority and structure to the church to lead it in worship. Although the true "senior pastor" is Jesus himself, Jesus calls under-shepherds to teach and protect and lead his flock. One term for these leaders is "elder," here in Acts 20:17, and "overseer" in 20:28 (see also 1 Tim. 3:1–7 and Titus 1:5–9).

Personal Implications

Take time to reflect on the implications of Acts 16:6–21:16 for your own life today. Consider what you have learned that might lead you to praise God, repent of sin, and trust in his gracious promises. Make notes below on the personal implications for your walk with the Lord of the (1) *Gospel Glimpses*, (2) *Whole-Bible Connections*, (3) *Theological Soundings*, and (4) this passage as a whole.

1. Gospel Glimpses

2. Whole-Bible Connections

3. Theological Soundings

4. Acts 15:36–21:16

As You Finish This Unit . . .

Take a moment now to ask for the Lord's blessing and help as you continue in this study of Acts. Take a moment also to look back through this unit of study, to reflect on some key things that the Lord may be teaching you—and perhaps to highlight and underline these things to review again in the future.

Definitions

[1] **Paganism** – Any belief system that does not acknowledge the God of the Bible as the one true God. Atheism, polytheism, pantheism, animism, and humanism, as well as numerous other religious systems, can all be classified as forms of paganism.

WEEK 11: THE GOSPEL GOES TO ROME

Acts 21:17–28:31

The Place of the Passage

Upon Paul's return to Jerusalem after his third missionary journey, he is confronted and attacked by some of the Jews. When he is arrested by the Roman tribunal, Paul begins a lengthy journey that ends in Rome, preaching the good news of the gospel with all boldness wherever he goes and to whomever he meets, from soldiers, sailors, and unreached tribes to governors and kings. Luke ends his account on a note of triumph, showing Paul in the capital of the world as he preaches the gospel "without hindrance" to all who will hear it (Acts 28:31).

The Big Picture

In Acts 21:17–28:31 Paul preaches the gospel without hindrance as the Lord uses him and his arrest to bring the gospel to Rome.

Reflection and Discussion

Read through the complete passage for this study, Acts 21:17–28:31. Then review the questions below concerning this section of Acts and write your notes on them. (For further background, see the *ESV Study Bible*, pages 2131–2145, or visit esv.org.)

Paul's visit with James in Acts 21:17–26 is another episode in the continuing struggle for many Jews to comprehend the spread of the gospel to the Gentiles. The word about Jesus scandalizes many Jews because it grafts Gentiles into the people of God without requiring them to abide by the law. We see Paul struggle with this issue throughout his letters, most especially in Galatians (Gal. 2:15–16, 19, 21; 3:2–3, 10–14, 19–25) and Romans (Rom. 3:21–26; 8:1–4; 9:30–33). Considering these passages, how is Paul unyielding about his obligation to spread the gospel to the Gentiles, and about their not having to keep the law?

We also see Paul doing all he can to demonstrate to the Jews that he values the law and its use for Jews, even undergoing these rites of purification (Acts 21:26). He encourages others to be flexible in nonessentials for the sake of harmony and humility in the church (see Romans 14). For the sake of spreading God's grace, Paul insists that he can become "all things to all people." Considering 1 Corinthians 9:19–23, how is Paul's undergoing the rites of purification a picture of allowing for adaptation of nonessentials for the sake of mission, without compromising the gospel or his identity in Christ?

Paul is convinced that God has called him to proclaim the gospel to all, despite the rejection he suffers. Read Luke 12:51–53. Considering Acts 22:22–29, how is Paul living out the persecution that Jesus promised would come to some of his followers when he foresaw that families would be bitterly divided on account of his kingdom?

In Acts 21:27–36, the Jews attack Paul and distort both what he said and what he did. How did they distort what Paul had to say? While the text doesn't always tell us the reasoning for accusations and attacks of others, what does the text say is the reason for the Jews' accusations here?

In Acts 22:1–23, Paul has another opportunity to preach the gospel before a Jewish crowd. Although he is interrupted before he can finish (v. 22), what is the result of Paul's declarations of his call to go to the Gentiles, and that God is concerned about them?

The Jews treasured their status as God's people, and found it difficult to accept that God was grafting in those from outside their race. Read Romans 11:11–24. How does this shed light on God's call to Paul in Acts 22:21?

_____

_____

_____

_____

_____

_____

_____

_____

In Acts 23:11, Jesus appears to Paul and encourages him to "Take courage." What does Jesus promise him? How do these words reflect his commission in Acts 1:8?

_____

_____

_____

_____

_____

_____

_____

_____

In Acts 28:14, Luke writes a brief geographical note: "and so we came to Rome." He ends Acts on a note of triumph, showing Paul in the capital of the world as he preaches the gospel with "boldness and without hindrance" to all who are willing to hear it (v. 31). Luke and Paul both knew that the mission that Christ had laid out had not been fully accomplished. Paul mentions in his letters that he intended to travel beyond Rome to even more distant Spain (Rom. 15:24). Considering Acts 1:8, how has Jesus already begun to fulfill his promise?

_____

_____

_____

_____

_____

_____

_____

_____

The triumphant march of the gospel mission in the book of Acts is detailed in several summary statements that Luke sprinkles throughout the narrative (Acts 2:47; 5:11, 14; 6:7; 9:31; 12:24; 13:49; 16:5; 19:20). How is Acts 28:30–31 a culmination of the gospel's advance in Acts?

Read through the following three sections on *Gospel Glimpses*, *Whole-Bible Connections*, and *Theological Soundings*. Then take time to consider the *Personal Implications* these sections may have for you.

▶ Gospel Glimpses

GOD IS THE DELIVERER. Luke goes into great detail about the storm at sea, in Acts 27:1–28:10. This account underscores a key theme: God can be trusted to fulfill his promises. The gospel will go to Rome and fulfill the promise of Acts 1:8 that Jesus' disciples would be his witnesses "to the end of the earth." God is the true actor behind the scenes. Paul acts as a messenger of God's promise, but he displays no power to quiet the storm, as Jesus did (Luke 8:22–25). Paul was first a recipient of God's grace, and now is an agent of grace to others, but God is the ultimate deliverer.

THE DEFEAT OF THE POWERS OF DARKNESS. In Acts 26:14–19 Paul includes additional details about his conversion. As Paul recounts, Jesus encapsulates his message as a call to turn from darkness and the power of Satan to the light of God that is manifest in the gospel of Christ. God's light has overcome Satan's darkness (John 1:5; 2 Cor. 4:3–6), even that darkness which inhabits us. God is sending a messenger to "open their eyes" (Acts 26:17–18). God offers defeat of the powers of darkness to those of us still under their control, not merely instructing us with self-help but washing away our sins and calling us to trust in Jesus (Col. 1:12–14; 2:15; 1 John 3:8). The "forgiveness of sins" is granted by faith in the name of Jesus (Acts 26:18), who died and rose again (Acts 26:23).

Whole-Bible Connections

RESPECT FOR GOD'S RULERS. Paul seems to be unaware that he has cursed the high priest in Acts 23:1–11, so when it is brought to his attention, he swiftly retracts. He still respects the office of the high priest, even when it is held by a man opposing him and the gospel. Compare this with David, who also respected a divine office—that of king—even when that office was held by a bad man, Saul. David intentionally avoided harming the Lord's anointed, even as Saul repeatedly attempted to kill him (1 Sam. 24:6). Obedience to God is seen in respect for his leaders, while resistance to God often manifests itself in resentment of them. Joseph's brothers despised him when he told them of God's plan to exalt him (Gen. 37:5–8). The Psalms equate rebellion against God's anointed with rebellion against him (Ps. 2:2). Jesus, as God's true Anointed One, was despised and executed because the people rejected his office (Luke 19:14; 20:14–18).

THE RESURRECTION. The central tenet of Paul's faith, and one that continually causes trouble throughout Acts, is the doctrine of Christ's resurrection (Acts 26:6–8). Paul bases his hope on God's raising of Jesus, which he sees as the final fulfillment of God's promises through the Law and the Prophets. For Paul, the resurrection of Jesus both confirms God's faithfulness and power to fulfill his promises, and provides the impetus for the spread of God's gospel and Spirit to Jews and Gentiles over all the earth (Acts 26:22–23). The resurrection was scorned in Athens (Acts 17:32) and frequently censured by the Jews. But Paul recognizes that the resurrection is the hope for which all of the Old Testament prophets waited and watched (Heb. 11:13, 39). God has always been about the business of bringing life from the dead, whether by creating life out of nothing (Gen. 1:1; Heb. 11:3) or by using his prophets to literally raise the dead (1 Kings 17:19–22; 2 Kings 4:34–35). Why, Paul asks, is it thought incredible that God raises the dead, when he has always had the power to do so? In the resurrection of Christ, God's power to raise the dead has been clearly manifested.

Theological Soundings

GOD'S PROVIDENCE. In Acts 25:9–12, we see a picture of God's creative sovereignty as God bends injustice for his good purposes. Paul is embroiled in a legal squabble that has kept him imprisoned in Caesarea for two years (Acts 24:27), while he yearns to bring the gospel to Rome (Acts 19:21). But in God's providence this convoluted legal squabble becomes the means for the gospel to reach Rome. When Festus attempts to transfer Paul out of his jurisdiction, Paul seizes the opportunity: taking advantage of his right as a Roman citizen,

Paul appeals directly to the emperor, guaranteeing a journey to Rome. It is unlikely that Paul initially anticipated that his journey to Rome would occur in chains. But Paul was confident that God would fulfill his promise (Acts 23:11), and knew that God's sovereignty works even through convoluted legal structures.

ANTINOMIANISM. The grace of the gospel frequently leads to the charge of antinomianism,[1] or lawlessness: that if grace is free, people will feel free to sin all they want. The first to levy such charges are, as here, those who are zealous to keep and compel religious commands. Paul goes to great lengths to satisfy the Jerusalem accusers, even accommodating James by submitting to a ritual Mosaic cleansing (Acts 21:26). Paul's opponents believed that people would try to keep God's commands only out of fear of punishment, and if that fear was removed, there would no longer be any motivation to live a righteous life. Into this situation comes news of the gospel, in which Jesus has removed the fear of punishment and freely reconciled us to God. Those zealous for the law can see only the potential danger: if Christians do not fear punishment, they will do whatever they want. The book of Acts refutes such accusations (compare Romans 6), showing that those who have experienced grace are motivated by remembering God's grace; because of God's great love for them, they do whatever he wants. They are compelled by the love of Christ (2 Cor. 5:14).

Personal Implications

Take time to reflect on the implications of Acts 21:17–28:31 for your own life today. Consider what you have learned that might lead you to praise God, repent of sin, and trust in his gracious promises. Make notes below on the personal implications for your walk with the Lord of the (1) *Gospel Glimpses*, (2) *Whole-Bible Connections*, (3) *Theological Soundings*, and (4) this passage as a whole.

1. Gospel Glimpses

2. Whole-Bible Connections

3. Theological Soundings

4. Acts 21:17–28:31

As You Finish This Unit . . .

Take a moment now to ask for the Lord's blessing and help as you continue in this study of Acts. Take a moment also to look back through this unit of study, to reflect on some key things that the Lord may be teaching you—and perhaps to highlight and underline these things to review again in the future.

Definitions

[1] **Antinomianism** – The false belief that OT moral laws are no longer necessary or binding for those living under grace (see Rom. 6:1–2).

Week 12: Summary and Conclusion

▲

We will conclude our study of Acts by reviewing and summarizing the big picture of Acts as a whole. Then we will consider a few questions for final reflection on Gospel Glimpses, Whole-Bible Connections, and Theological Soundings, all with a view to appreciating the book of Acts in its entirety.

The Big Picture of Acts

The book of Acts is a story about God's grace flooding out into the world through the gospel. In Acts 1:8 Jesus promises a geographic expansion through the power of the Holy Spirit. In Acts 2 the church is given the gift and empowerment of the Holy Spirit, and the rest of Acts records the result as the good news of Jesus' death and resurrection spreads from a small, uneducated, fear-filled group of disciples in Jerusalem to Judea, Samaria, Asia, and finally to Rome. Acts has many characters, but ultimately Acts is a story about a single main character: it is the account of the continuing work of God through Jesus, by the power of the Holy Spirit.

The last lines in Acts say that Paul is proclaiming Jesus "without hindrance" (Acts 28:31). Paul is under house arrest in Rome and has faced fierce opposition, yet through it all the gospel continues to advance into the entire world. This last phrase, "without hindrance," leaves us hanging on for more of the story, and invites us to participate in God's mission as he overcomes opposition to bring his word of forgiveness to all people.

The church does many things, but Acts is not centered upon what the church does. It is not a book about evangelism, discipleship, church leadership, or missions as such. Acts reminds us that we are caught up in God's work, in his story. The gospel is God's good news that will go out, regardless of the obstacles and oppositions. The church is God's people, his witnesses to his powerful work of redemption through Jesus Christ.

Read through the following three sections on *Gospel Glimpses*, *Whole-Bible Connections*, and *Theological Soundings*. Then take time to consider the *Personal Implications* these sections may have for you.

▶ Gospel Glimpses

Acts reveals God's passionate pursuit of his people, beginning with his followers in Jerusalem, expanding to Samaria, then to the rest of the world. The gospel draws people in, constitutes them as the church centered on the grace of Jesus, and then sends them out in mission to the world. Each new group of believers is marked by the Holy Spirit, who creates such a distinctive community that others are drawn in, experiencing God's grace. At the same time, they take the gospel message to new people and new lands, making God's grace known to the ends of the earth. Acts makes clear that no one is beyond the scope of God's saving power, nor is anyone exempt from the need for God's redeeming grace. All people receive the grace of God through one man, Jesus Christ. Jesus' gospel goes out to all places and all types of people, because Jesus is Lord of all.

Has Acts brought new clarity to your understanding of the grace of God? If so, how?

_____

_____

_____

_____

_____

_____

_____

_____

_____

Were there any particular passages or themes in Acts that brought the gospel home to you in a fresh way?

_____

_____

_____

_____

_____

_____

_____

_____

_____

Whole-Bible Connections

Acts shows that the new Christian movement is not a fringe sect, but the culmination of God's plan of redemption. The gospel's expansion is the culmination of what God has been doing since the beginning. Luke consistently grounds salvation in the ancient purpose of God, which comes to fruition at God's own initiative. This reveals God to be the great benefactor who pours out blessings on all people (Acts 2:17, 21). Even the capacity to repent is God's gift (Acts 5:31; 11:18). What was seen only as shadows in the Old Testament, God reveals finally and fully through Jesus Christ. The book of Acts does not primarily provide us with human patterns to emulate or avoid. Instead, it repeatedly calls us to reflect upon the work of God, fulfilled in Jesus Christ, establishing the church by the power of the Holy Spirit.

How has this study of Acts helped shape your understanding of the redemptive work of God throughout the biblical story line?

Were there any biblical connections that you made through Acts that you hadn't noticed before?

Did your study of Acts help you to understand the culture and values of the New Testament world a little better? If so, how?

What development has there been in your view of who Jesus is and how he fulfills the Old Testament?

Theological Soundings

Acts contributes much to Christian theology. Doctrines that are reinforced and clarified in Acts include law and grace, justification by faith, divine sovereignty, the deity of Christ, and the work of the Holy Spirit.

Has your theology been shaped or changed as you have studied Acts? Why? How?

_____

_____

_____

_____

_____

_____

_____

_____

How does Acts uniquely contribute to your understanding of God, creation, humanity, and Jesus?

_____

_____

_____

_____

_____

_____

_____

_____

What theological themes struck you the most in Acts?

_____

_____

_____

_____

_____

_____

_____

_____

Personal Implications

As you consider Acts as a whole, what implications do you see for your own life? Consider especially the grace of God. This is an important emphasis throughout Acts. In Acts, "grace" is a parallel for "the gospel" or "salvation." Jesus' message is summarized as "the word of his grace" and "the grace of the Lord Jesus" (Acts 14:3; 15:11; 20:32). Believers are said to have received "grace" or to be "full of grace," and they are challenged to continue in "grace" (Acts 4:33; 6:8; 11:23; 13:43; 15:11; 20:24). The missionaries in Acts proclaim the grace of God, and it is through this grace that people are able to respond with faith (Acts 14:3, 26; 15:40; 18:27; 20:24, 32). What are the ramifications for your own life of the grace of God as revealed in Acts?

As You Finish Studying Acts . . .

We rejoice with you as you finish studying the book of Acts! May this study become part of your Christian walk of faith, day by day and week by week throughout all your life. Now we would greatly encourage you to continue to study the Word of God on a week-by-week basis. To continue your study of the Bible, we would encourage you to consider other books in the *Knowing the Bible* series, and to visit www.knowingthebibleseries.org.

Lastly, take a moment again to look back through this book of Acts, which you have explored during these recent weeks. Review again the notes that you have written, and the things that you have highlighted or underlined. Reflect again on the key themes that the Lord has been teaching you about himself and about his Word. May these things become a treasure for you throughout your life—which we pray will be true for you, in the name of the Father, and the Son, and the Holy Spirit. Amen.